The Grenada Documents:
Window on Totalitarianism

Nicholas Dujmović

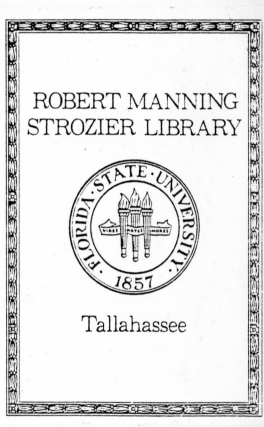

Special Report
1988

A Publication of the
INSTITUTE FOR FOREIGN POLICY ANALYSIS, INC.
Cambridge, Massachusetts, and Washington, D.C.

PERGAMON · BRASSEY'S
International Defense Publishers

Washington London New York Oxford Toronto Sydney Frankfurt

Pergamon Press Offices:

U.S.A.
(Editorial)

Pergamon-Brassey's International Defense Publishers,
8000 Westpark Drive, 4th floor, McLean, Virginia 22102

(Orders & Inquiries)

Pergamon Press, Maxwell House, Fairview Park,
Elmsford, New York 10523, U.S.A.

U.K.
(Editorial)

Brassey's Defence Publishers,
24 Gray's Inn Road, London WC1X 8HR

(Orders & Enquiries)

Brassey's Defence Publishers,
Headington Hill Hall, Oxford OX3 0BW, England

**PEOPLE'S REPUBLIC
OF CHINA**

Pergamon Press, Qianmen Hotel, Beijing,
People's Republic of China

**FEDERAL REPUBLIC
OF GERMANY**

Pergamon Press, Hammerweg 6,
D-6242 Kronberg, Federal Republic of Germany

BRAZIL

Pergamon Editora, Rua Eça de Queiros, 346,
CEP 04011, São Paulo, Brazil

AUSTRALIA

Pergamon Press (Aust.) Pty., P.O. Box 544
Potts Point, NSW 2011, Australia

JAPAN

Pergamon Press, 8th Floor, Matsuoka Central Building,
1-7-1 Nishishinjuku, Shinjuku-ku, Tokyo 160, Japan

CANADA

Pergamon Press Canada, Suite 104, 150 Consumers Road,
Willowdale, Ontario M2J 1P9, Canada

Library of Congress Cataloging-in-Publication Data

Dujmović, Nicholas, 1958—
The Grenada Documents.

(Special report/Institute for Foreign Policy Analysis)
1. Grenada—Politics and government—1974. 2. New Jewel Movement (Grenada)—History.
3. Totalitarianism. I. Title. II. Series: Special report (Institute for Foreign Policy Analysis).
F2056.8.D85 1987 972.98'45 87-32514
ISBN 0-08-035969-8 (pbk.)

First Printing 1988
Printed by Corporate Press, Inc., Washington, D.C.

Contents

Preface

Among the numerous benefits to the United States resulting from the military operation that ousted a Marxist, Soviet client government in Grenada was a wealth of documentary materials. This special dividend in itself furnished ample evidence of the strategies and tactics by which a small Caribbean island state, having only recently achieved independence, was co-opted by the Soviet Union and gradually pushed toward totalitarian rule. As such, the present work furnishes numerous insights into the process by which Soviet client states have been created in the Third World. It affords an understanding of the broader geostrategic significance attached to Grenada by the Soviet Union. In light of the ongoing commitment of the Institute to the publication of analyses of Soviet strategy and policy, the present work represents a contribution to a broader understanding of the dynamics of revolutionary behavior and the application of Marxist-Leninist principles to a Third World situation, together with implications for U.S. policy and what has been termed the Reagan Doctrine.

Robert L. Pfaltzgraff, Jr.
President
Institute for Foreign Policy Analysis

Summary Overview

Whether one considers the U.S.-led invasion of Grenada in October 1983 a Normandy-style "liberation" or "Yankee imperialist intervention," the historical significance of the event is undeniable if only because of the resulting disclosure of the Grenada Documents. Representing virtually all of the paperwork generated in the four and a half years of the People's Revolutionary Government (PRG), this enormous amount of material offers a rare view into the workings of a Third World Marxist-Leninist state. Specifically, the Documents can give Western scholars, students, and decisionmakers needed insight regarding the development of totalitarianism in countries vulnerable to Soviet or Cuban influence.

It is the socio-political system termed "totalitarianism" by political scientists and historians which is the analytical model chosen for this evaluation of the Grenada Documents. Although the totalitarian state is, quite fortunately, a rare occurrence in history, much academic debate has centered on this twentieth-century phenomenon. Scholars generally have agreed on the following characteristics by which a totalitarian regime may be identified and distinguished from the traditional authoritarian dictatorship:

- an absolute, messianic ideology;
- a single, strict, hierarchical party under one leader;
- a commitment to engineer a "new man" in the "new society";
- population control through secret police and the military, both instruments of the party;
- societal mobilization and reeducation through party control of all media, education and cultural organizations;
- a centralized economy; and,
- a tendency toward expansionism.

Scholars such as Carl Friedrich and Zbigniew Brzezinski have observed that, while traditional dictatorships (or *authoritarian* regimes) may possess one or more of these characteristics, only *totalitarian* states exhibit all these traits.

Totalitarian leaders such as Hitler or Lenin recognized that party and ideology each could not exist without the other. The party receives from the ideology its *raison d'etre*, its guidance, and its justification for any extreme means; at the same time the party prevents the totalitarian ideology from being merely an intellectual exercise. In Grenada, it was the development of the New Jewel Movement (NJM) from its origins as a West Indian black power group into a pro-Soviet, ideologically committed, Marxist-Leninist party that gave the first indications of a growing totalitarianism destined eventually to seize power in this Caribbean island and capture the attention of the world.

Maurice Bishop, the charismatic Grenadian lawyer who would become the NJM's "Comrade Leader," started his political activism in the 1960s with his study of the writings of Martin Luther King, Jr., and Malcolm X. The Documents indicate, however, that by 1970 Bishop had begun to incorporate Marxism in his thinking and Leninist tactics in his methods.

In its 1973 *Manifesto* the NJM called for the transformation of Grenada into a "new society" for the "new Grenadian man" free of outmoded values. At the same time the NJM, acting through front organizations, called for the violent overthrow of the existing government and its replacement by a "vanguard." The Documents show that through the 1970s the NJM increased its ties to Cuba, set the Party firmly on a Marxist-Leninist foundation, and planned to oust Eric Gairy, Grenada's Duvalier-like leader, by force.

After the March 1979 coup (inaccurately but deliberately touted by the NJM as a mass-based revolution), the NJM abolished the Grenadian Constitution and Parliament as "undemocratic." The Party also placed all broadcast media under its control and took steps to centralize the Grenadian economy.

To provide a facade of accountability, the NJM established citizen assemblies for public discussions with NJM leaders. In actuality, however, the NJM used these meetings merely to judge the mood of the masses, and to determine if Party political work should be intensified in a particular locale. Elections were promised but never held, and the evidence is unequivocal that the primary goal of the NJM was to keep itself in power. Minutes of NJM Central Committee meetings, for example, show that discussions of proposed elections and the constitutional commission focused not on their intrinsic merits, but rather on how they could be controlled by the Party. Opposition parties, promised freedom in the 1973 *Manifesto*, were effectively forbidden under NJM rule. Attempts to organize political opposition were broken up by NJM goons who were allegedly exercising their own "democratic rights" (in a manner identical to the *turbas divinas* of the Sandinistas).

The NJM regarded a free and independent press in the same light as democratic ideals or political pluralism, that is, it was not to be tolerated. The archives confirm that the Party could scarcely have cared less about the alleged "CIA connection" by which media shutdowns were justified;

rather, the Party simply did not believe in press freedom. Again in a style reminiscent of the Sandinistas, the NJM first harassed and then closed down the independent, anti-NJM newspaper, as well as the Roman Catholic newsletter. When an opposition newspaper emerged after meeting the strict and discouraging legal requirements established by the PRG, the organizers were arrested, the equipment was seized, and the paper was shut down after only one issue. The NJM itself endeavored to operate as a classic Leninist party in accordance with the principle of "democratic centralism," and demanded the utmost loyalty from its elite membership. Party members were required to sacrifice personal resources and time, and attendance at frequent ideological training sessions was mandatory. This training, involving study of the works of Marx, Lenin, and Stalin, was designed to raise political consciousness and "to fight superstition and the lingering belief in God." Lessons were often taught by the highest Party leaders, including Bishop and Bernard Coard. Ideological training was also provided abroad to selected Grenadians who studied in the USSR, Cuba, East Germany, and Bulgaria.

In one of the more illuminating documents, a secret speech to the Party membership, Bishop assured his "comrades" that "we have hegemonic control on power" and made it clear that only the Party determined the scope of individual freedoms. Bishop declared that the NJM represented the will of the majority; all those who disagreed with this majority were members of the bourgeois minority and, said Bishop, "the majority will crush, oppress, and repress the recalcitrant minority."

The NJM's main instrument in maintaining power was the People's Revolutionary Army (PRA), considered by the Party to be its "sword and shield." PRA recruits were immersed in political indoctrination, often by Cuban instructors, and the PRA acted as a totalitarian secret police with broad powers of search and arrest. The PRA provided bodyguards for the NJM leadership; and, significantly, political prisoners were in PRA rather than police custody.

For monitoring potential sources of "counterrevolution," especially the Catholic Church, the NJM employed Special Branch, a small but very active police organization which acted as the eyes and ears of the Party. Special Branch maintained a permanent "watch list" on all possible "counters" and conducted extensive surveillance (including intercepting mail) on farmers' groups, unions, student organizations, and every aspect of church activity, especially sermons. Special Branch infiltrated any Grenadian organization not under NJM control and even sent agents abroad to report on Grenadian emigre communities.

Political prisoners, euphemistically called "detainees" by the regime, comprised the vast majority of the prison population. With few legal rights, political prisoners were held, and sometimes tortured, for months or even years without being charged or even questioned. At one point approximately one of every 300 Grenadians was imprisoned; later reductions in the prison population were the result of international diplomatic pressure. Those released were forced to sign a confession as well as a "Voluntary Declaration," a legally binding promise to assist the PRG authorities by reporting all "subversive activities."

The police and prison systems of the PRG were targeted for significant organizational, operational, and ideological improvements provided by the Soviet Union and its network of surrogate and client states. Cuba, for example, trained PRG police in both criminology and Marxism-Leninism. East Germany provided technical assistance in electronic and telephonic surveillance. At the time of Operation Urgent Fury, Vietnam was advising the NJM on reeducation techniques pursuant to a planned "pickup" of the leadership of the island's Rastafarian community, and twenty Grenadian security personnel were to be trained by Vietnam in the "reeducation of anti-social and counter-revolutionary elements."

Like any totalitarian party, the NJM attempted to replace all previously existing relationships between individuals with the single relationship permitted in the new order—that between the individual and the party. The totalitarian party, already masquerading as a state, continues the charade as the media, a sports club, or even the Church, but the end remains the same: no loyalties are permitted, except to the party. Using a coordinated orchestration of Party-controlled organizations, the NJM attempted to create this "New Grenadian" of the appropriate political consciousness, loyal only to the Party. The NJM maintained in every district an agitation and propaganda machine to "mobilize the masses" in support of the regime, to condemn U.S. imperialism, and to celebrate special holidays, such as Lenin's birthday. Once the potential opposition press was eliminated, the Grenadian people had as information sources only the eight NJM newspapers, the PRG television and radio stations, and the official PRG news agency, all coordinated by the State Propaganda Committee, an arm of the Party. The "progressive" ideological slant given to all news and information was deliberately and consistently pro-Soviet and anti-U.S. Advance copies of newspapers and programming schedules were meticulously checked by Bishop and Coard to make sure that the political message transmitted to the masses was sufficiently "agitational" and "served the revolution." As always, the network of "fraternal" socialist states assisted the NJM in its efforts. Cuba provided a 50-kilowatt radio transmitter and trained PRG media technicians. East Germany, Romania, and the Soviet Union provided journalism scholarships. The Soviet Union's TASS office in St. George's was a constant source of well-written, ideologically sound material for the PRG media.

Totalitarian regimes place great emphasis on the country's youth in the process of creating the new society promised by the ideology. The NJM had a two-pronged program, involving both formal education and extra-curricular organizations, to reeducate the children of Grenada. The Party's Education Committee oversaw the standardization of school curricula along political lines, the island's cultural activities, and even the showing of films in the moviehouses. By replacing "right wing" principals—mostly those who headed Christian private schools—with "democratic and progressive replacements," by nationalizing private schools, and by including in the standard curriculum political indoctrination disguised as "civics," the Party came close to achieving its stated goal of "total state ownership and control of all educational institutions."

In addition to developing political training in the school system, the NJM mobilized thousands of children in the Young Pioneers, that quasi-military political organization already known to countless Soviet and Cuban youngsters. A similar organization was run by the NJM for teenagers and young adults, who were admonished that "youth must take positive steps in promoting revolutionary culture." Through Pioneer camps, social activities, military drills and political indoctrination, the Party aimed to include every Grenadian child in this loyal cadre and "to creatively raise the anti-imperialist consciousness of the Pioneers and to step up the involvement of children in building the Revolution."

As the self-defined "vanguard of the working class," the NJM could not oppose the independent unions; the Party, therefore, pledged itself to the eventual takeover of the unions to effect the "organizational and ideological control of the working class." Unions were infiltrated by NJM members, and union leaders were co-opted by the Party or intimidated into submission. By the end of 1981 Party hegemony over the unions was complete, and Bishop proudly stated that their leadership had been "thrown into the dustbin of history."

Despite the PRG's claim that religion in Grenada had never known more freedom than under its benevolent rule, all churches in Grenada were subject to government interference, and religion was identified by the Party as the primary obstacle in the eventual transformation of society. In addition, the churches' support of individual freedoms, and especially their concern for prisoners of conscience, made religion an immediate political enemy of the NJM. The Party attempted to remove "the Christian syndrome into which young minds are being locked" through the manipulation of the school day and the curriculum, the removal of "backward" teachers, and the takeover of religious schools; the Party considered religion anathema to its agenda because it "extract[s] the child, in particular, from the context of the Revolution." To an even greater degree, the PRA was free, in Lenin's words, of "every idea of God"; soldiers were cautioned that religious activity was "counterrevolutionary." With the assistance of Cuban intelligence, Special Branch regularly monitored sermons for political context; clerics were routinely followed, and an agent even infiltrated a Catholic rectory to watch the priests. The Documents indicate that Bishop was planning to establish, with Nicaraguan and Cuban help, a "progressive" church based on the Marxist theology of liberation and therefore pliant to the will of the Party.

To the New Jewel Movement, even Grenadian culture was considered an ideological instrument with which to forge the new society. In accordance with the slogan "Culture is Warfare," the Party endeavored to give all cultural activities a specific political message so that the population would develop a "revolutionary cultural consciousness." Its monopoly over the country's mass media enabled the Party to present to the people a constant barrage of ideologically correct music, drama, and dance. Young Pioneers as young as five or six would learn children's songs which were denunciations of imperialism. Revolutionary songs were taught to soldiers and union members. Citizen assemblies resembled Orwellian hate sessions, with "people's poets" whipping the attendees into an anti-U.S. frenzy. The NJM saw no intrinsic value in cultural activities themselves; culture's worth was solely dependent on its revolutionary context.

The totalitarian ideology of Marxism-Leninism aims toward full control of the economy because, to the Marxist-Leninist, life *is* economics; the transformation of society is impossible if the populace still exercises bourgeois economic freedoms. Although the NJM initially hesitated from exercising complete state ownership of property and control of the economy, this reticence was recognized as part of a transition period similar to Lenin's New Economic Policy (NEP); Bishop made clear to the Party membership that both free enterprise and a mixed economy were rejected as the NJM's ultimate economic goal. Total state ownership and control, Bishop said, was impossible "for the time being" because of a lack of an industrial infrastructure and the small size of the working class. Nevertheless, the PRG, in accordance with the NJM plan, nationalized all utilities, banks, insurance companies, transportation facilities, and the tourist industry. The Soviet bloc provided major assistance both in industrialization and in the extensive training required to run a centralized economy.

It is in the area of agriculture that the Documents reveal most clearly the totalitarian bent of the New Jewel Movement. Pending the development of an industrial base, the Party recognized that economic centralization must of necessity focus on agriculture. Not only was the collectivization of agriculture ideologically consistent, but the Party also regarded collectivization as a practical instrument in eliminating the expected opposition to its policies. Toward the eventual goal of complete state ownership of land, the Party surveyed about one-third of Grenada's farmland for nationalization, including acreage "which now belongs to the most hostile elements of the landed bourgeoisie." This "idle land" was seized in 1982, and the Party planned completely to "transform the countryside" by late 1985, thereby effecting the "modernization of agriculture and the total destruction of the landowning class." Though the Party fully expected a hostile reaction to its land policy, the Documents indicate the price the NJM, like any totalitarian party, was willing to pay to accomplish its objectives. The Party discussed at length the "strategy and tactics . . . we have for crushing the Grenada Kulaks." Elsewhere, the Party resolved that "they will have to be smashed." The use in the Grenada of the 1980s of the Russian word "kulak"—a euphemism for Soviet genocide in the early 1930s—illustrates the fungibility of totalitarianism's evils.

Through the previous publication of excerpts of the Grenada archives, the development of the PRG's armed forces into a formidable regional threat is well known. Together with the completion of the infamous airport, Grenada was being turned into a significant logistics and operations resource for Cuba and the Soviet Union, one which could have created major complications for U.S. decisionmakers responding to a crisis in Europe. The most important immediate role assigned by Moscow to the NJM, however, was as a center for training regional Marxist-Leninist parties, Caribbean leftist fringe groups which hoped to repeat the NJM experience. With Cuban assistance, the NJM sponsored conferences at which the region's leftist parties participated in workshops on general propaganda techniques, agitation in trade unions, creation of mass organizations, and "Leninist administration." The ideological and organizational development of these parties was accompanied by the growth of the NJM's military arm, the PRA, so that armed support of a Leninist coup was possible. This was the NJM's contribution to the expansion of totalitarianism in the Caribbean region.

The lessons of the Grenada experience for U.S. hemispheric policy are unambiguous. On balance, Grenada under the New Jewel Movement was in intention and direction a totalitarian state. By itself, this conclusion is of academic interest, but there are important implications which make Grenada more than an historical curiosity. Only from Grenada is there such a complete window on the inner workings of Third World, Soviet-supported totalitarianism. If the United States is truly interested in "no more Grenadas," then the Documents have great relevance for U.S. decisionmakers as well as for scholars.

Today in Central America, a totalitarian movement under the sponsorship of the Soviet Union and Cuba is simultaneously trying to consolidate its power fully in Nicaragua, and to foment unrest throughout the region, so that all Central America might be united under its ideology. Although there is as yet no "Sandinista archive," the available evidence points to the totalitarian nature of the FSLN. By implication, we can expect not only that the

Nicaraguan people will suffer to a greater degree than under the merely authoritarian Somoza if the FSLN is left alone; we may also conclude that Nicaragua's neighbors, and ultimately the United States, are in danger.

Its leadership of the Grenada invasion notwithstanding, the United States has a poor track record in identifying and confronting totalitarianism. The Grenada Documents should be used to educate the public and the Congress of the United States in the basics of totalitarian theory, so that the totalitarian nature of the Sandinistas will be evident. This will help create the needed and presently lacking consensus on U.S. policy toward Central America.

Introduction: The Documents as History

The U.S.-led invasion of Grenada in October 1983 has been described by many conservative thinkers as a unique event in the history of what Richard Nixon calls "the Real War"—that is, the struggle between a system based on individual freedom and a system based on collective domination, between liberty and totalitarianism, between capitalism and communism, indeed, as the argument runs, between good and evil. Grenada represents to many the first (and so far the only) instance in which a society subdued by a Communist-dominated, Soviet-supported government has been liberated from without, shattering once and for all the Brezhnev Doctrine's claim of irreversibility. To others, of course, the invasion was not the liberation of a newly subjugated people; rather, it was yet another in a long series of actions by the United States to expand its control of the region and thereby stand between an already oppressed nation and its legitimate aspirations to a life of greater political and economic freedom.

Regardless of one's political interpretation—"liberation" or "Yankee imperialist intervention"—the historical importance of the event is undeniable if only because of its disclosure of what are now known as the Grenada Documents. An enormous amount of material—representing virtually the entire body of paperwork produced by the People's Revolutionary Government (PRG) in its four-and-a-half years of existence—the Grenada Documents offer a rare view into the inner workings of a Leninist state. Scholars such as Jiri and Virginia Valenta have pointed out that only twice before have comparable documents from communist regimes been made available in the West to students of such governments; they refer, of course, to the Smolensk Archive from World War II and the Czechoslovak Communist Party archives made available by the events of 1968.[1]

The Grenada Documents, however, stand alone in their historical importance. They are unique for several reasons. First, the Documents speak of events that are nearly as contemporary as the evening news. The Grenadian Revolution—its rise, decline, and demise—is so immediate to our own day that objective analysis seems hindered by a lack of perspective. Collected as a sheer mass—with no regard for subject matter, politics, or (to the scholar's chagrin) any organization whatsoever—the Grenada Documents can provide needed analytical distance. Second, the Documents are our

---

[1] Jiri and Virginia Valenta, "Leninism in Grenada," *Problems of Communism* 33 (July-August 1984).

only window thus far opened onto the landscape of a relatively new and potentially dangerous political entity, namely, the Third World Marxist-Leninist state, serving as a loyal member of the Soviet/Cuban network of clients. The study of these Documents can give both scholars and decision makers insights rarely available into the nature and intentions of other members of this "club," such as the People's Democratic Republic of Yemen, the MPLA government of Angola, and the Sandinista regime in Managua. Third, virtually all the Documents are in English, making this huge body of primary source material accessible to any interested scholar or student in this country. Though the unfamiliar Caribbean usages and nonstandard spelling may at times be confusing (not having been marked *sic* at every juncture), it is hoped that instructors of history, international relations, and political science will recognize the classroom potential of the Grenada Documents. (Want to gain an understanding of the practical goals of an elite Leninist Party? Read Maurice Bishop's confidential "Line of March" speech of September 1982, Document 12203.[2])

Finally, the Grenada Documents are unique simply because of the size of the archive. Even after laying aside the material of only marginal interest, the Documents are roughly twice as extensive as those that comprise the Smolensk Archive. Interested scholars may peruse all of the estimated 500,000 pages of material (on microfiche) at the National Archives; fortunately, there are also several good edited selections of the Documents available. The most extensive work is a U.S. government publication edited by Herbert Romerstein and Michael Ledeen, *Grenada Documents: An Overview and Selection*. Also good is *The Grenada Papers*, edited by Paul Seabury and Walter A. McDougall. This volume includes a learned analysis written by the editors. Two recent works which place the Grenada Documents firmly in the framework of Soviet geostrategy are *Hydra of Carnage*, edited by Uri Ra'anan, et al.; and the particularly useful collection of essays edited by Jiri Valenta and Herbert J. Ellison, *Grenada and Soviet/Cuban Policy*.

These selections, though helpful in bringing some of the more sensational of the Grenada Documents to the public's attention, are nevertheless lacking in two areas. First, due to the simple limitations of time and physical manageability, no collection provides an analysis based on more than a small fraction of the entire body of material. What is lacking is an analysis based on a comprehensive survey of the Documents. Second, because they focus on the international implications of the Grenadian Revolution, these works cannot offer an overall conceptual framework through which the interested student can place the Grenadian Revolution in political perspective. Presumably, the United States would prefer "no more Grenadas."

---

[2] Document 12203, Bishop's "Line of March" speech to the Party, 13 September 1982. This is one of the most illuminating of the Grenada Documents.

If so, then what is needed is an analysis based on a "unified field theory" approach, grounded in political theory, which will assist the student or strategist in determining whether "another Grenada" is in the offing.

This present work attempts to rectify these shortcomings of earlier treatments of the Grenada Documents. It is based on extensive research; in the three months the author enjoyed exclusive access to one set of the Documents, more than half of the material was reviewed. Important documents were brought to light through this work, as yet unnoticed by other researchers.

The analytical model chosen to organize and evaluate this tremendous volume of data is the socio-political system termed "totalitarianism" by political scientists and historians. This is certainly not the first assessment of Grenada under the New Jewel Movement (NJM) as a totalitarian state. In public pronouncements prior to Operation Urgent Fury, President Reagan often characterized Grenada as a totalitarian state on the Cuban model, which endangered the Caribbean region with the potential export of its political system. Seabury and McDougall claim in their book that the documents demonstrate conclusively "the making of a totalitarian state." Others have echoed this sentiment, and have gone so far as to say that in launching the operation the United States finally acted to "roll back" totalitarianism for the first time since World War II. Though there can be little doubt from the published selections of the documents that Grenada in the period 1979 to 1983 was an increasingly oppressive society with a complex series of ties to the Soviet bloc and Cuba, to level the charge of totalitarianism at this tiny spice-producing Caribbean tourist trap is, to the historian, a grave accusation. Indeed, repressive, authoritarian police states are all too common in the world, but the very word "totalitarian" conjures up images of gas chambers, the Gulag, "killing fields," omnipotent secret police, and a society of fear. A totalitarian state is not just a system of physical control; Stalin was not just a Soviet Shah, nor was Marcos a Pol Pot. The concept of totalitarianism goes far beyond authoritarianism, as Walter Laqueur observes in a recent *Commentary* article:

Every dictatorship or semi-dictatorship is *a priori* authoritarian, be it a monarchy (Saudi Arabia, Jordan under Hussein, Morocco under Hassan) or such a disparate regimes as Pakistan, Vietnam, and Indonesia, not to mention all African and most Latin American countries . . . Of what use is a category which can be applied to nine-tenths if not more of the member states of the United Nations?[3]

Totalitarianism suggests a tyranny over mind as well as over body, and implies an evil greater than that of traditional dictatorships.

The concept of totalitarianism is an old one; Plato's *Republic* provides useful guidance to any would-be totalitarian. Dostoevsky's Grand Inquisitor from *The Brothers Karamazov* and Turgenev's nihilist Bazarov from *Fathers*

---

[3] Walter Laqueur, "Is There Now, or Has There Ever Been, Such a Thing as Totalitarianism?" *Commentary* 80:4 (October 1985).

3

and Sons are 19th century literary manifestations of totalitarian thought. The emergence of totalitarianism as an actual form of government, however, was only made possible by 20th century technology coupled with absolute, messianic ideologies. The unprecedented oppression, and other similarities, between Nazi Germany and Stalin's USSR provoked serious postwar discussion on the characteristics of totalitarian systems. Since the late 1940s, the available literature on the phenomenon of totalitarianism has blossomed, and scholars have engaged in much heated debate over the essential nature of the beast.

Definitions of totalitarianism seem to vary as widely as definitions of democracy or justice. Nevertheless, there are certain characteristics on which a consensus is enjoyed among most writers on the subject. These include:

- An absolute or totalist ideology, messianic in nature, which both purports to explain history and promises to bring happiness and peace to man.

- A single party, usually under one leader, with a strict, hierarchical organization.

- A commitment to the development of a "new man," free of the outdated, corrupt values of the previous order.

- Control of the population through the party's monopoly of the armed forces and secret police.

- Mobilization of the masses through the party's control of all cultural, media, and information systems, including the educational system.

- A centralized economy, which serves to strengthen the party's control over society.

- Expansionism. As "keepers of the flame," a totalitarian party feels compelled to bring all mankind to the wisdom of its ideology.

It is hoped that the reader will keep these seven characteristics in mind when examining the following material on the People's Revolutionary Government of Grenada, 1979-1983.[4]

In the first chapter, the ideological and organizational development of the NJM is traced. The Party's attitude toward traditional Western democratic freedoms is described, as well as its use of the military and security services as instruments of control. The second chapter analyzes the relationship between the Grenadian population and the NJM, which claimed

---

[4] Those wishing to learn more about the study of totalitarianism are directed to Carl Friedrich and Zbigniew Brzezinski's *Dictatorships and Autocracy* (Cambridge: Harvard University Press, 1956), or Hannah Arendt's seminal *Origins of Totalitarianism* (New York: Harcourt Brace Jovanovich, new edition 1973). A recent and important interpretation of totalitarianism as a counterculture is Jeane Kirkpatrick's essay, "Reflections on Totalitarianism," in her *Dictatorships and Double Standards* (New York: Simon and Schuster, 1982).

to be a "vanguard Party"; this section specifically addresses propaganda, reeducation, and manipulation of what Gaetano Mosca called the "social forces" of a people. The third chapter deals with the Party's approach to economics, and the fourth chapter is a discussion of the degree to which the Party intended to impose its ideological convictions beyond the beaches of Grenada.

In the footnotes, references to Grenada Documents are made simply by "Document 00000," followed by a description of the document; if the actual title is given, it is enclosed in quotation marks. Cross-references to published documents are also provided in specific cases. Throughout, I have endeavored to support conclusions with the corroboration of several documents, or with material from news sources and speeches made by the PRG leadership.

1. The Party: Ideology and Instruments

Central to any concept of totalitarianism is the existence of a party as the organizational manifestation of whichever ideology is proclaimed as the one true faith. The goal of the totalitarian party is not unlike that of any political party, that is, to gain power in order to implement its ideology. What makes the totalitarian party distinct from other forms of political organizations are the strategy and tactics it utilizes to pursue this objective. The totalitarian ideology, the grand strategy of the party, is the mother lode of all knowledge, from which derives the tactics involved in taking and maintaining power. Like the concept of the party, ideology is a necessary ingredient of any totalitarian model; indeed, it can be said that party and ideology are different expressions of the same essence, one operational, the other theoretical. It is certain that one cannot exist without the other. A totalitarian ideology without a party is at its most energetic an intellectual exercise, a fact obvious to the imprisoned Adolf Hitler working on *Mein Kampf.* A totalitarian party without an ideology is a contradiction in terms. Like a ship without a rudder, it is not properly a ship at all; such vessels prefer the static, authoritarian existence of a firm anchorage in a familiar harbor.

Lenin provided the means by which the ideology, or his version of it, could be transformed into political power. Lenin did not invent the small, underground party; but through the force of his personality, his party was successful in attaining and maintaining power. It became the paradigm for party leaders such as Mussolini, and later Hitler. Lenin insisted on a few standard operating procedures for party structure and discipline which later became tenets of Marxism-Leninism, and which in fact were strictly followed by subsequent totalitarian parties.

First, the party would be a professional, revolutionary vanguard, an elite acting as the enlightened trustee of the proletarian masses whose lower consciousness prevents them from knowing when to take revolutionary action on their own. Immediately, then, we see an elitist arrogance of purpose combined with profound cynicism, even disdain, for the masses. Second, Lenin insisted that the Bolshevik Party adhere to the "principle of democratic centralism." The party leader is the interpreter of the ideology, ordained by history and always knowing the correct path. Discussion may be allowed, but all decisions are final and not subject to debate. Dissidents suffer from the "false consciousness" of the corrupt, overthrown society, and may be dispatched to the ash-heap of history.

Finally, because it aims at eliminating the corrupt structure of society, the party must engage in deception to camouflage its genuine goals until it has achieved state power. In the pre-revolutionary period this means adopting some of the structure, activities, and rhetoric of conventional political parties. Though it intends to do away with these decadent bourgeois trappings, the party plays the bourgeois game in order not to be recognized as the threat to existing society that it is. Once it takes power, the party, now in the guise of a legitimate government, must continue an outward program of deception so that the international community does not recognize the threat posed by the inherently expansionist totalitarian state. In general, a totalitarian party finds it politically expedient and ideologically obligatory to mask its nature from any potential threat, domestic or foreign.

Development and Pre-Coup Activity of the New Jewel Movement

The history of the formation, pre-coup political activity, and finally the rule of the New Jewel Movement (NJM) is the story of the transformation of a West Indian black power group—initially limited in its outlook to greater popular political participation in a country the size of an average U.S. town—into a pro-Soviet, ideologically orthodox Marxist-Leninist party. Once transformed, the movement staged a successful *putsch* and managed, through its regional and international activities, to draw the attention of the world.

The Grenadian revolutionary tradition in this century dates from the 1920s and 1930s, when the labor unrest which shook much of the industrialized world also jolted the West Indies. A significant regional figure in the 1930s was a Grenadian, Uriah Butler, who led labor demonstrations in the oilfields of Trinidad. Grenada itself had no industry to speak of, but there was a large and generally destitute agricultural work force; over 70% of the arable land was held by less than 5% of the land owners. Land reform and the breakup of many large estates in the 1940s led to an increase in the number of peasants, while the development of the sugar, nutmeg, and coffee "agro-industries" increased the opportunities for collective organization of what Grenada's Marxist rulers would later call the "agro-proletariat." The low standard of living suffered by most Grenadians, combined with the rising expectations produced by the formation of unions and cooperatives, ensured that labor unrest continued to be commonplace into the 1950s. Eric Gairy first gained national stature with his leadership in the general strikes of 1951. As the head of an important trade union, his successful contest of the elections that year brought him and his party (the Grenada United Labour Party, or GULP) into power, a reign which saw independence for the island in 1974, and which was virtually unbroken until the NJM coup of March 1979. GULP won five of the seven elections between 1950 and 1972. At no time did GULP win a majority of votes; it continued in power through a combination of electoral manipulation, the disunity of the opposition, and Gairy's considerable charismatic attraction with his largely illiterate constituency.

Like Marcos of the Philippines, Gairy built a political system based on patronage and favoritism. Like the Duvaliers of Haiti, Gairy intimidated the opposition with a personal corps of loyal thugs, his "Mongoose Gang." Like any traditional authoritarian ruler, Gairy wanted to command a static, apolitical society. Unlike any totalitarian, he was not in the social engineering business; his only ideology was to further his own interests. Gairy's concern for the people seemed genuine, if misguided: though his Mongoose hoodlums might chop off the hands of those distributing an illegal opposition pamphlet, Gairy appeared to be convinced that the Grenadian people were content even in their poverty. He also claimed a divine mandate to rule; in one radio broadcast Gairy said that "I have been appointed by God," implying that the NJM opposed the "divine plan."[5] There was enough popular enthusiasm and support for "Uncle Gairy" to reassure him that the authentic Grenadian people loved him (though not the communist New Jewelers, whom Gairy took a special interest in persecuting) and that no major changes were needed in the levels of political and economic participation for the majority of Grenadians.

In societies where a privileged and seemingly immovable elite exists side by side with the mechanics of an ostensibly democratic polity, idealistic young dissidents feel morally justified in opposing the system by both legal and extra-legal means. It is a form of unconscious emulation of the current political elite: using the facade of the system, going through the motions of the democratic process, while at the same time relying on the extra-legal means available to attain one's aims. For the existing elite, the goal is to keep power; for the challengers, it is to attain power. The optimum mix of legal and extra-legal means depends, of course, on operational capabilities as well as the limitations imposed by the political environment. However, the struggle of those who would be king requires a plan, an ideology, which gives at least an indication to the sub-elites and rank-and-file of the direction of the movement, and which provides the discipline necessary to carry the movement through difficult times.

Maurice Bishop began his political activities in the 1960s with his study of the writings of civil rights activists such as Martin Luther King and black power advocates such as Malcolm X (whose mother was from Grenada). Bishop was a good public speaker and, in the beginning, a regular churchgoer. In 1963 he spoke, for example, at a patrician meeting on "The Catholic Viewpoint on Re-armament." There is no evidence that suggests a commitment to any particular ideology prior to his departure for England in 1964, to study law and to work. It was in London that Bishop began to look beyond black nationalism, which was the prime vehicle of West Indian political dissent. Between his jobs at a tax office and at a legal aid society representing London's West Indians, Bishop studied Julius Nyerere's African socialism and the writings of the Caribbean Marxist C. L. R. James.

---

[5] *Newsweek*, 14 February 1974. See also *Time*, 2 April 1979.

Upon his return to Grenada in 1970, Bishop immediately began to put his developing ideology—at this point still more black-oriented than Marxist in nature—into practice. He started a black nationalist discussion group, Forum, similar to groups in St. Lucia and St. Vincent. In Grenada, however, Bishop led Forum from discussion to political activism. Forum organized political marches to protest the corruption of Gairy's government, while Bishop himself provided legal defense for protesters arrested during demonstrations. Despite these activities, the group never attracted more than a few supporters; this was probably due to a combination of general political apathy in Grenadian society, the genuinely widespread support Gairy still commanded with the people, and fear of the "Mongoose Gang" among those who might have joined.

Forum distributed a weekly newspaper of the same name which openly criticized Gairy and his policies. Like the group, *Forum* did not receive much attention (except from Gairy himself), but surviving issues are worthy of note. Editions of *Forum* from July 1970 reveal Bishop's ideological evolution. The newsletter featured a weekly series on Marxism; one issue declared that

... the strongest and most vital force in the struggle to better the life of man has come, not from Christian institutions but from the followers of Karl Marx.[6]

This statement is significant for two reasons. First, in a deeply religious country Bishop wisely refrained from taking an unequivocally atheistic line or otherwise attacking religion directly; instead, he criticizes "Christian institutions," that is, the Church. Once in power, the NJM would broaden its antipathy to organized religion into a consistently Marxist attack on religion itself.

Second, the statement gives credit not to Karl Marx himself, but to unidentified "followers" of Marx. The suggestion that Bishop was studying Lenin at this early date is absent from the available literature, but is given credence both by this reference to "the followers of Karl Marx" and by an essay Bishop wrote in 1970. In this essay Bishop used a Leninist-like argument, reminiscent of the "Draft Editorial Resolution for *Iskra*" (1900), in advocating the establishment of an independent newspaper to further the ideals of Forum. Unlike its above-ground namesake, however, this new paper, the *Spark* (not coincidentally the English translation of Lenin's *Iskra* masthead) was to be an underground journal. In fact, *Spark*'s 1970s masthead was identical to that of *Iskra* in 1900: "A Spark shall kindle a Flame." When this underground publication finally appeared after the NJM

---

[6] Document 12190: *Forum*, 17 July 1970.

was formed in 1973, *Spark* took a far more revolutionary stance than *Forum* or its successors; for this reason, articles were unattributed and any connection to Bishop's group was denied.[7]

Forum folded for want of popular support, so Bishop tried again by regrouping under a new name, the Movement for the Advancement of Community Effort (or MACE), which he led with the future PRG Minister of Legal Affairs, Kenrick Radix. MACE's stated goal was to conduct research into the problems of Grenadian society, and then to educate the masses with its findings. By this two-stage process, it was hoped, change would be initiated. MACE was an indication of Bishop's growing awareness that political change in Grenada required a mass-based organization. MACE soon gave way to MAP, the Movement for Assembly of the Peoples, also led by Bishop and Radix. MAP abandoned MACE's research aims and became openly political; Bishop and Radix stated that their aim was the attainment of state power and the transformation of Grenada's Westminster-style government into one more directly controlled by the population. The ideological direction of MAP was more or less along socialist lines, but it still lacked focus.

MAP's intellectual image did not gain it many supporters in the Grenadian countryside, where there were other opposition groups at work. In March 1972 a political debate group merged with a cultural appreciation group to form JEWEL, the Joint Endeavour for Welfare, Education and Liberation, under the leadership of a returning Howard University student, Unison Whiteman. Whiteman was later to be Bishop's foreign minister and fellow victim of the Coard faction. Predominantly rural-oriented, JEWEL's object was to undermine Gairy's support in the countryside, among the so-called "agro-proletariat," by using socialist arguments for greater economic equity. Given both the commonalities of aim and ideological leanings, it is not surprising that MAP and JEWEL merged in March 1973. This had the effect of giving the more elitist MAP a semblance of a rural base, while strengthening, through mutual reinforcement, the developing leftist ideology. This latter incarnation of Bishop's original Forum group was called the New Jewel Movement, or NJM.

The period between the March 1973 formation of the New Jewel Movement (hereafter referred to as NJM, or the Party) and the *putsch* of March 1979 was characterized by both an increasing commitment to Marxist-Leninist ideology, and a continuing and consistent denial of any communist orientation. Bishop told the Cuban magazine *Bohemia* that the NJM began studying Marx and scientific socialism in 1974. A 1982 Party document indicated that the decision to make NJM a Marxist-Leninist party was made

---

[7] Document 11843: Bishop paper on the *Spark*, 1970. Compare with Lenin's "Draft Editorial Resolution" of 1900, *Collected Works* (Moscow, 1960), Vol. IV, p.320.

in April 1974. A close reading of the Party's *Manifesto* of March 1973, however, reveals that the NJM was already planning more than a socialist redistribution of political and economic opportunity. The *Manifesto* stated the NJM's objective as a completely socialist economy (including the radical restructuring of agriculture into "co-operatives") free from exploitation by foreign capitalism, and a social welfare system which would guarantee food, housing, and employment for all. The political order was to be transformed from the inequitable parliamentary system of representation into one of direct popular participation through the dual mechanism of people's and worker's assemblies: this transformation was to be effected by a provisional government consisting of all existing political factions, including Gairy's party, "without regard to favor." Specifically, the NJM rejected the party system as divisive and undemocratic:

We feel that no small group of persons, regardless of how intelligent or educated or wealthy they are, have the right to sit down together in a small room and proclaim themselves the new Messiahs.[8]

In the same document, however, the NJM proclaims itself "the people's choice," implying that no other group truly represents the general will. Finally, the seeds of totalitarianism emerge: the *Manifesto* states that under NJM leadership, a "new society" would be created, where "an entirely new system of values" would operate; a "new man" would emerge, who would reject prior political and economic consciousness. "The creation of this new man demands the transformation of the minds and hearts of each and every one of us."

Though the *Manifesto* reveals the totalitarian Marxist orientation of the NJM's goals, it does not explicitly indicate a Leninist method for taking power; on the question of getting from here to there, the NJM was deliberately vague. The Documents make clear, however, that peaceful evolution to the "new society" was rejected by the Party in favor of the brute seizure of power. In 1974 Bernard Coard formed a secret study group within the NJM called the Organization for Research, Education and Liberation (OREL); its purpose was to promote a more consistent Marxist-Leninist line within the Party. Officially, OREL was a separate political group, and any connection with the NJM was denied, both in NJM's weekly, the *New Jewel*, and in OREL's publication, the *Spark*. This denial was made necessary by virtue of the *Spark*'s advocacy of violent revolution as the only means of political change in Grenada. OREL also implied that its perspective was the only correct one, and that if necessary the people would have to be forced to be free. For example, one issue of the *Spark* stated:

---

[8] NJM *Manifesto* of March 1973, reprinted in *Caribbean Monthly Bulletin* (hereafter *CMB*), Institute of Caribbean Studies, University of Puerto Rico, April 1979, pp.26-53. See also Document 11710: "Development of the Subjective Factor (Brief History of Party Development)," September 1982 (hereafter, "History of Party Development") and Document 10374: Pre-coup NJM papers. These documents refute the view of Cole Blaiser and others that the NJM was driven to socialism by an ideologically hostile United States.

The masses must be *made to understand* the treachery of Gairy . . . They will therefore be prepared to accept and/or support what must logically follow, seeing the need for the *violent* overthrow of the rich ruling class.[9]

OREL not only described itself as the result of an evolution from black nationalism to scientific socialism (racism was but one manifestation of capitalism), but considered itself a "vanguard movement" in the struggle to overthrow the rule of the bourgeoisie. In the *Spark*, the NJM was identified as the only mass-based revolutionary movement capable of changing society and putting power in the hands of the workers; all other groups suffered from "miserable self-deception" (that is, false consciousness).[10]

Because it was actually an elitist group aiming at the violent overthrow of the existing order, it was expedient for the NJM to conceal its true nature while it continued the charade of a traditional party pursuing political change through established and legal means. With two other opposition parties the NJM formed the People's Alliance coalition in November 1976, the purpose of which was to defeat Gairy's GULP in the general elections of December. The Alliance failed in this attempt, but the NJM gained another medium of protest by winning three of the 15 seats in Parliament, and Maurice Bishop became the leader of the "loyal" opposition. At the same time, the NJM continued its open espousal of transforming Grenada into a socialist paradise, while its front group OREL advocated violent means to achieve this end. NJM's political image was not enhanced by the May 1977 visit of Bishop and Whiteman to Cuba for consultations with Castro, though apparently the visit quelled any remaining dissent within the Party over the full adoption of Marxism-Leninism. By mid-1978, the NJM connection with OREL was becoming apparent, the Party was being accused by Gairy of being communist, and even the other members of the Alliance began to distance themselves from it. At that time the NJM began to moderate its public statements and avoid the harsher socialist rhetoric. The Party came out with a new publication, *Exposure*, in which it denied that it was interested in political domination; NJM's commitment to the People's Alliance was claimed to be solid. The Party rejected as "undemocratic" calls to denounce OREL, and avoided charges that it was a communist group.

We have repeatedly stressed that we are *Socialists* determined to move our country on to a socialist oriented path . . . Those who wish to form different views and attach labels of communists are free to do so. We are satisfied that the people will not be diverted, confused or misled by labels, witch-hunting or anti-communist hysteria . . . let it be

---

[9] See Documents 10016, 10670: *Spark*, various editions, 1974-1975; emphasis added.

[10] For Coard's long-standing Marxist-Leninist perspective, see Document 11897: "The Political Economy of Underdevelopment," Coard paper, 30 January 1967. OREL seemed a unique acronym since MACE, MAP, and JEWEL all mean something in English. OREL, however, is Russian for "eagle."

clearly stated that we in the NJM are NOT anti-communist. We recognize, appreciate and applaud the tremendous contribution made by the Soviet Union, Cuba and the Socialist World system to the cause of the oppressed the world over.[11]

Elsewhere, the NJM flatly denied that it was a communist movement, though "some Marxist analysis is valid." Yet in reality, the Party leadership had not only decided on a Marxist-Leninist foundation, but was actively planning a coup. An internal Party memorandum lists certain requirements for revolution, including positive central control of the Party, agitation among the masses as the "primary and material basis for defeating anti-c[ommunism]," and intelligence collection throughout the country. By these means, the memo states, the Party will have the

Capacity to secure and consolidate state power in all areas and regions of the country in an immediate post-G[airy] situation. . . .

Capacity to supervise, control and implement economic and political decisions of a post-G rev. govt. in a rev. manner.[12]

By March 13, 1979, when the "post-Gairy revolutionary government" was established, the NJM was a Marxist-Leninist, pro-Soviet communist party, acting as the sole interpreters of the will of the people, with no internal restraints on its goal of remaking Grenadian society.

The NJM: After The Coup

As it is not the purpose of this paper to investigate the mechanics of the U.S. invasion of October 1983, likewise it is not the intent to investigate the overthrow of the Gairy government in March 1979 by the NJM, except as it relates to totalitarianism. It has been shown that the mechanism for the takeover was in place; all that was needed was a pretext. For purposes of the present study it will suffice to say that while Gairy was out of the country, Bishop and his colleagues claimed that the Mongoose Gang had been ordered to murder the NJM leadership in Gairy's absence.

That the operation of 13 March 1979 was an elite coup rather than a genuine revolution is confirmed by observers of the event, including the Grenadian correspondent Alistair Hughes, at that time an NJM supporter and friend of Maurice Bishop. Hughes reports that 54 members of NJM's military arm, the People's Revolutionary Army (PRA), effected the coup in 35 minutes. Letters of congratulations from Grenadians, genuinely happy to see Gairy's government fall, refer to nothing but the "victory of NJM," the "coup," the "coup d'etat," "your victory," "your overthrow"; even NJM members and Bishop's

---

[11] Document 10399: "NJM Replies to Torchlight," August or September 1978. See also Document 11600: *Exposure*, 28 August 1978. Document 11610: Pamphlet "ABC's of NJM," 1977. *CMB*, October 1978, p.6.

[12] Document 9314: "What will systematic organisation of our Party groups in every part of the country bring us?" pre-coup NJM memo. See also Document 11710: "History of Party Development," September 1982.

friends recognized the "brilliant success" of the NJM. There were virtually no references made by Grenadians on-scene to a popular revolution, simply because they had not observed one. The new government, however, immediately began to tout the coup as a mass-based revolution. For example, a pamphlet widely distributed one month later declared that it was a popular revolution and not a coup d'etat that had occurred: the NJM had merely acted on behalf of the Grenadian people.[13]

It was allegedly on behalf of the people that the NJM's People's Revolutionary Government (PRG) immediately began to implement the provisions of its 1973 *Manifesto* regarding the socialist transformation of Grenada's economy and society. The details of these will be discussed later. On the political level, however, it must be noted that the NJM's initial actions were directed at restricting dissent. The Constitution and Parliament were abolished, as promised, and in their place were established assemblies of workers and citizens, in zones within each parish.* These Zonal and Workers Councils were, in effect, large "rap sessions" at which the people could talk with PRG or Party leaders; there was, however, no system of representation or established accountability. In addition, the PRG immediately nationalized the broadcast media; the non-PRG print media were allowed to operate for the time being.

The post-coup NJM exhibited characteristics of an elite totalitarian party. Unlike a traditional authoritarian regime which merges state and party, the NJM deliberately remained separate and distinct from the government; in fact, the PRG was nothing but a facade, an instrument of the Party. The Party structure paralleled that of the government; Party members filled every important government position. As Bishop reported in a confidential speech to a general meeting of the NJM,

There is absolutely no doubt that we have hegemonic control on power and over all capital areas of the State . . . and over 90% direct control by the Party of the ruling council of the P.R.G. and Cabinet.[14]

Furthermore, Bishop stated, "bourgeois elements"—that is, persons not approved by the Party—were excluded from leadership positions in the military, trade unions, and Zonal and Workers Councils.

Within the Party, members were expected to devote their whole being to the needs of the Party, subordinating their personal lives to its needs. Dissent was not allowed; all decisions were handed down from the Politburo and

---

* Grenada is organized politically into six parishes.

[13] "Reports by Alistair Hughes," *CMB*, April 1979. Documents 2132, 2133: Congratulatory Letters to Bishop. Documents 2153/103301: Pamphlet "One Month After the People's Revolution."

[14] Document 12203: Bishop's confidential speech to the NJM membership, "Line of March for the Party," 13 September 1982. For Party-state parallelism, compare the PRG structure in *CMB*, September 1981 with Document 10557: Committees of the NJM.

Central Committee to the general membership in accordance with the Leninist principle of "democratic centralism," and sworn loyalty to the Party and its leadership was obligatory. Party members were required to watch each other and grade each other's commitment to the Party in a form of socialist competition called "emulation." Attendance at all Party functions and training sessions was mandatory, and infractions were dealt with by the Party's Disciplinary Committee, headed by Party ideologist Bernard Coard. Party members were required to hand over 5% of their gross monthly income. The children of NJM members could attend only government schools; the use of private schools was "a contradiction to the line of the Party." The Party reserved the right to control a member's physical activities, including both exercise and rest. Bishop admonished Party members that they had to exhibit "a complete willingness to accept Party discipline . . . Being a Communist, comrades, means becoming a different kind of person."[15]

Self-criticism, the totalitarian "cult of confession" observed by psychologist Robert Jay Lifton, was required of all members. Self-criticism was an ubiquitous element of all Party committee meetings, especially when the goals of the Party were not being met. It was almost considered a magic panacea for any failure or shortcoming; self-purging of bourgeois attitudes would purify the Party and ensure its success. "Comradely" criticism and self-criticism was always directed at the individual; the Party itself was considered free from any fault. Addressing the "revolutionary principle" of self-criticism, the Party's youth organization stressed that

We must in every way seek to ensure that Petty-bourgeoisie [sic] ideas and attitudes do not seep out into our ranks but that our Revolutionary working class ideas and attitudes remain of the purest kind.[16]

The best summary of the type of "new proletarian person" sought by the Party is provided by the following questionnaire for applicants to Party membership. All questions are listed:

How do you see our Revolution of March 13?

Are you satisfied that our Leaders are working for the common good of all Grenadians?

What do you think of COMRADE MAURICE BISHOP as a REVOLUTIONARY LEADER?

Are you prepared to defend the Revolution, even at the cost of your own life?

---

[15] "Line of March" speech, ibid. Document 6869: "Minutes of Meeting Held With the New Applicants to the Party," 5 January 1982. Document 8212: NJM Politburo directive regarding school for NJM members' children, 7 September 1983. Document 2381: NJM Code of Conduct.

[16] Document 9314: "Criticism and Self-Criticism," undated paper of NJM's National Youth Organization. For more examples of comradely self-criticism, see minutes of the NJM Central Committee, Documents 2183/000184, 2109/00123, 9924, and 11786. See also Robert Jay Lifton, *Thought Reform and the Psychology of Totalism* (New York: Norton, 1961), pp.419-436.

Do you consider the Leadership of our Revolution as pillars of Revolutionary process?

Are you prepared to defend and protect them?

Even with your own life?

What class do you see our Revolutionary Government fighting for?

Are you prepared to fight against EXPLOITATION OF MAN BY MAN?[17]

Becoming a member of the Party was a three-stage process that normally took two years to complete. Applicant members underwent a six-month course of study primarily designed to develop the perspective that Marxism-Leninism "is not an abstract science but that it is a guide for the working class in the struggle for socialism . . . being a Communist is not simply a matter of accepting ML theoretically." For three hours per week applicants would study Marx and Lenin, the history of the class struggle, class definitions, and the new society to be established by the dictatorship of the proletariat.

In the next stage, that of candidate membership, study would continue with political economics, dialectical materialism, and the history of both the Communist Party of the Soviet Union and the world working class movement. Lest these budding Party members get carried away with the promises of the ideology and forget the realities of political power, it was important for candidates "to fight idealist conceptions in philosophy, political economy, and scientific Communism." Candidates were warned that, while the capitalist system might look "natural," all instruments of capitalism (including churches, schools, and the media) have a "backward" (that is, false) consciousness, and that only a Leninist vanguard party could lead the struggle against this backwardness.

Finally, the training did not stop with full Party membership; study continued with historical and dialectical materialism, the "main aim [being] to fight superstition and the lingering belief in God." The NJM Code of Conduct required every Party member to study socialist, communist, or "progressive" literature for one hour per day, and one three-hour study session at the Party office per week. Party members not conversant in the ideology were required to attend weekend seminars and "crash courses" in Marxism-Leninism. While the works of Marx and Engels, Mao, Kautsky, and Dmitrov were standard fare, the emphasis was predominantly on admiration of the Soviet experience. The study of Lenin's works was stressed by Bishop; a great admirer of Lenin, Bishop referred to him as "a man of impeccable moral character" who had "infinite love for the working people." (It is probably no accident that Bishop named his son Vladimir.) Coard, on the other hand, preferred Stalin and would use both the *Dialectics* and

---

[17] Document 8845: "Political Rating Questionnaire" for NJM applicants, classified Confidential.

Foundations of Leninism when he led courses in Marxism-Leninism. In addition, literature on such communist "leading figures" as Felix Dzerzhinsky and Zhdanov was required.[18]

Ideological training was provided in quantity by the Soviet bloc. At least 14 Grenadian students attended Patrice Lumumba University in Moscow, where they received instruction in the "Historic Experience of the CPSU," the "World Communist Movement," and "Social Psychology and Propaganda." Twenty-one more Grenadians were known to attend "Higher Party Schools" in the USSR, Cuba, and East Germany. Bulgaria provided 24 scholarships for the five-month course of the Bulgarian Communist Party school.[19]

The training and development of a Party member was a task that was taken seriously by the NJM. The required ideological commitment was complete, and the sacrifices were expected to be high. Despite the obvious shortage of Party members—virtually all had to do double and triple duty, with both NJM and PRG assignments—and despite the support given by the Soviet bloc, the New Jewel Movement remained among one of the most elite ruling parties in the world. Three months before the end of the PRG, the membership of the Party, including members who were ambassadors abroad, stood at just 65—less than 0.06% of the population.[20]

The People's Revolutionary Army: Sword and Shield of the Party

The documents found in Grenada also indicate that the People's Revolutionary Army (PRA) as a whole was trained in Marxist-Leninist ideology. Although there were only 17 full Party members in a regular force of about 3000, the PRA was considered the "sword and shield" of the Party, and as such received much political indoctrination.

The first objective in recruit training was the political preparation of the recruit with respect to the PRA's role "in the defense of the Revolution"; weapons training, physical fitness, and military drills were secondary aspects in the development of the PRA soldier. Every company commander

---

[18] Document 9681: "The Leninist Party of the Working Class," Lecture 3 in the Candidate Study Course. Document 11733: "Proposals on Course for Three Levels of Party Members," undated. Document 2381: NJM Code of Conduct. Document 2292/100288: Minutes of NJM Organizing Committee regarding weekend training course, 3 May 1983. Document 2025/00184: NJM Central Committee minutes regarding Coard-led crash course, 12-15 October 1982. Document 10663: "Lists of Books for Study Groups." Document 6117: Draft Bishop speech for the 113th anniversary of Lenin's birth.

[19] Document 3482: Evaluations on Grenadian students in the USSR. Document 2291/100278: NJM Organizing Committee minutes regarding ideological training abroad, 20 June 1983. Document 7121: Letter from Bulgarian Embassy in Havana to PRG Embassy, 4 May 1981.

[20] Document 2345/110498: NJM membership list, July 1983. For comparison, four years after the Bolshevik Revolution, Communist Party strength was about 4 percent of the RSFSR population.

had a second-in-command that was listed on the rosters as "political commissar"; this individual was most often an applicant or candidate member of the Party, and was responsible for the ideological consciousness of the troops. PRA troops were mobilized at political rallies, both to provide protection for the NJM leadership and to help agitate the masses with their own revolutionary enthusiasm and hatred for capitalism, cultivated at the frequent ideological study sessions. It is clear that some of the training received from Cuban military instructors in Grenada was ideological in nature. Soldiers were taught the Marxist-Leninist perspective on just and unjust wars, revolutionary wars, and wars of national liberation; they received instruction on the arms race "caused by imperialism," and were told that detente took second place to the "proletarian assistance" provided by socialist countries so that poor peoples could become "victorious over imperialism." Bishop himself exhorted the troops never to forget that "imperialism never relaxes." PRA units celebrated fraternal holidays such as the anniversaries of the founding of SWAPO and the PLO; the commemoration of the Bay of Pigs; and the celebration of Lenin's birthday (to which a full week was devoted). According to the Party, the purpose of the constant ideological barrage was:

. . . to prepare them to have undying love for their homeland and to be prepared to die in defending the motherland and revolution.

. . . that patriotism that will lead comrades to make that ultimate sacrifice can only be maintained and developed with the ever increasing and living political work.[21]

Party cadre in the PRA (about 90, including applicants and candidates) were required to take the following oath:

I Pledge:—

To always carry high the banner of the Party and of my socialist ideology and conviction.

To always display and support Iron discipline in the Armed Forces understanding that victory over Imperialism cannot be accomplished without it.

To constantly strive to raise my ideological level.

To assist in raising the Political, Cultural and Combative level of my Comrades. . . .

I say let the whole contempt and hatred of the Party and working people fall upon me if I display cowardice, opportunism or in any way disgrace the name of the Party and endanger the cause of Revolution.[22]

The political training was effective, and ensured PRA unity in the final crisis. By September of 1983 all the failures of the Party's economic and mass mobilization campaigns were blamed on the lack of Leninist qualities in the "comrade leader" Maurice Bishop. Youth organizations, the militia, and the economy were falling apart. Bernard Coard, Bishop's chief rival, had

---

[21] Document 11733: "Mass Political Education in the Army," undated.
[22] Document 6647: PRA Party cadre oath.

resigned the previous year from the Politiburo and Central Committee because, he said, the Party lacked the requisite Leninist discipline. Coard also wanted to impress on the Party membership as a whole his great worth as both a theoretician and practical leader, thereby making his return inevitable. In October Coard's allies in both bodies, who had been with him in OREL and were now primarily the top leadership in the PRA, suggested a plan for joint leadership of the Party and country: Bishop would represent the country as prime minister and head the Central Committee, while Coard would head the Politburo. The rest of the Central Committee, at a loss for a solution to the potential disintegration of the Party, approved the resolution for joint leadership. At first Bishop agreed to this plan, but soon after returning from a trip to Cuba he made known his doubts. The PRA promptly issued a proclamation.

... we call on the Central Committee and the entire Party to expel from the Party's ranks all elements who do not submit to, uphold and implement in practice the decision of the Central Committee and Party membership but are bent on holding up the Party's work and spreading anti-Party propaganda ... LONG LIVE THE PARTY—NJM! LONG LIVE LENINISM! LONG LIVE THE PEOPLE'S REVOLUTION![23]

Security personnel were told by top PRA officers not to take orders from Bishop personally, but only from the Central Committee, the only authentic representative of the working class. Bishop was arrested, but was soon set free by a crowd of Grenadians distrustful of Coard's faction. PRA troops obeyed their orders and attacked the defenseless crowd protecting Bishop. After the execution of Bishop and several followers, a military dictatorship was established. A 24-hour curfew was imposed and Grenadians were told that "lumpen elements" had tried to protect the "counterrevolutionary, criminal opportunist elements" of Bishop, Whiteman, and the others. Bishop was declared to be a traitor to socialism—"he was going to build a new Party and a new Army to defend the interests of the bourgeois." The PRA was the true defender of the Revolution; as in Hungary in 1956, Czechoslovakia in 1968, and Poland in 1981, the army fulfilled its duty to save the Party.

All patriots and revolutionaries will never forget this day when counter-revolution, the friends of imperialism were crushed ... SOCIALISM OR DEATH!!![24]

Despite the radical rhetoric, the PRA quickly disbanded when faced with the overwhelming firepower and numbers of the invasion forces.

In one major respect the relationship between the NJM and the PRA does not correspond to the totalitarian experience. As Hannah Arendt notes, in totalitarian systems the secret police are given the place of honor ahead of the military as the defender of the movement. Grenada under the PRG did

---

[23] Document 2012/00298: PRA proclamation, 19 October 1983.

[24] Document 2051/00298: PRA Bulletin, 20 October 1983. For an eyewitness account of the final days, see Hugh O'Shaughnessy, Grenada (New York: Dodd, Mead, 1984).

have a small secret police force, the activities of which will be discussed later; but the "Special Branch" was clearly subordinate in prestige to the PRA and, it is nearly certain, took no steps to penetrate it. In many ways the PRA acted as a secret police; from the first days of the regime, the PRA had police powers of arrest and search, later broadened to make warrants unnecessary. The PRA and not the Prison Service guarded political prisoners. If Bishop had enlarged the size and scope of Special Branch to the point where it became a rival of the PRA for the attention of the Party—and identified the person of Bishop with the Revolution—he would have been better equipped to prevail in the power struggle of September and October 1983.[25]

Politics, Democracy, and the Press:
The Approach of the People's Revolutionary Government

This we regard as a very serious violation of the rights of Parliamentarians and a serious abuse of the workings of Parliament.

> —*Opposition Leader Maurice Bishop in 1977,*
> *regarding a four-month delay in presenting*
> *the budget.*[26]

It has been argued by many—generally by apologists for Maurice Bishop and his "genuine" movement—that the Coard faction represented a betrayal of the Revolution; once the Revolution had been consolidated, the argument runs, Bishop was planning to replace the NJM's strongarm measures with his own ideals of a free and just society, including a Constitution, free elections, a genuinely free press, and so forth. Because the Coard faction was as much devoted to liberty (and was therefore as much an aberration) as Stalin, Bishop and his supporters had to be eliminated. Unfortunately for this view, there is no evidence that Bishop differed much in his political outlook from his colleagues, even those who would ultimately have him murdered. As Herb Romerstein and Michael Ledeen have concluded, there is no evidence to suggest that the power struggle was based on anything but personal considerations.[27]

---

[25] Many other documents refer to the political indoctrination of the PRA and its use as a Party instrument. Noteworthy are the following: Document 2299, Planning document for PRA 8-week Recruit Training Course, undated; Document 2453/100690, "Existence of Party Cadres in the Armed Forces," classified Secret, 23 September 1983; Document 2276, Notes of 2nd LT Michael George, June-July 1983; Document 2297, PRA Training Report, 14 March 1983. (For Bishop's speech to the PRA, see *CMB*, March 1982, p.25.) Also of interest are Document 2325, PRA Political Program, 1982-1983; and Document 6916, CPT Stroude letter to PRA Party cadre, 27 April 1982.

[26] *CMB*, April-May 1977, p.3.

[27] Apologists include O'Shaughnessy, pp.227-228; and Jay R. Mandle, *Big Revolution, Small Country* (Lanham, Md.: North-South Publishing, 1985). Herbert Romerstein and Michael Ledeen, editors, *Grenada Documents: An Overview and Selection* (Washington, D.C.: USGPO, September 1984), pp.14-15.

The earliest document of the new People's Revolutionary Government yet to be identified is an internal memorandum on the first communique of the new government, and was probably written in the first hours of the PRG. Significantly, it focuses on Western opinion of the coup with respect to human rights and democratic government, and not on the intrinsic merits of these issues. The document notes that caution is required because

this is the first major political statement from the Revolution, therefore it will be meticulously analyzed by Foreign Ministries throughout the world (particularly the State Department of the U.S.A.). . . .

Because the question for all will be "Is the Revolution Communistic?" the first official statement should make

Particular reference to security of private property, individual rights . . . Whether traditional human rights (in the Western sense) be protected or might the people expect their violation by 'communistic' totalitarianism. . . .

The memo recommends instead that emphasis be made on "Gairy's totalitarian rule" and

The discovery of the order by Gairy to assassinate the leadership of the New Jewel Movement. (Is Affidavit obtainable?)

Finally, the document recommends that the PRG promise "The return to constitutional rule at the earliest possible opportunity . . . Free and fair elections under the People's Constitution." This was the line declared by Bishop the first day on "Radio Free Grenada," at a press conference three days after the coup, and at a rally held two weeks later.[28]

The first acts of the PRG were the abolition of both the Grenadian Constitution and the Parliament. The government subsequently legitimized itself by People's Law Number One in which, predictably, the PRG was declared the result of the choice of the Grenadian people. Periodically throughout the four-and-a-half year life of the PRG, when pressed for details by foreign journalists or politicians, Bishop would declare that yes, both a constitution and free elections were in the future, but it was impossible to say when; in fact, he argued, the Grenadian people themselves were not in favor of elections in the near future. At an August 1979 press conference, for example, Bishop declared that "the people of Grenada did not have a revolution to have an election, but to see the country reconstructed."

. . . the predominant response and impression we get is of people who are telling us, 'Forget elections for 10 years,' 'Forget elections for 20 years,' . . . We believe that the majority of

---

[28] Document 10404: "Suggested Form and Content for Major (1st) Statement," undated but almost certainly 13 March 1979. See Bishop's radio address in *Maurice Bishop Speaks* (New York: Pathfinder Press, 1983). See also *CMB*, April 1979.

patriotic Grenadians are concerned about consolidating the revolution . . . it is ludicrous to talk of elections next week or next month . . . We are not concerned that, in theory, there is no Constitution on paper. . . .[29]

The lack of concern for a constitution is confirmed by a concomitant lack of discussion on the matter in the minutes of the PRG cabinet, as well as the NJM Politburo and Central Committee meetings. It is known that the PRG announced in mid-1983 the formation of a commission to study the establishment of a People's Constitution, but the view of the NJM leadership on the meaning of a constitution is shown by the minutes of a Central Committee plenary; the discussion focused, not on the intrinsic merits of a constitution, but on how it provided "moral legitimacy and prestige" with the masses—this statement from Bishop himself. The Central Committee also discussed the question of "how will we be able to maintain and control these structures." Because it was believed that many Party members might hold bourgeois ideals regarding the purpose of a constitution, the Central Committee agreed that a purge of the Party would be necessary before the Party discussed the constitution at the First Party Congress, scheduled for November 1985.[30]

As with the matter of a constitution, the issue of free elections seems not to have concerned the NJM leadership except insofar as the process could be controlled. An agent sent to observe the Jamaican elections of May 1980 reported to the Politburo that there was enough evidence of fraud in Seaga's defeat of leftist Prime Minister Manley that the PRG could use this as an excuse to postpone elections in Grenada. Lloyd Noel, the PRG Attorney General, authored a report on establishing an "election infrastructure" subject to Party control. The Party would dictate to the parishes the requisite "qualifications and expectations" on nominations; these nominees would be subject to approval by a Party Election Bureau which

reserve[s] the discretionary measure of selecting a suitable Candidate for a Constituency where it considers the suggested person not up to scratch. . . .[31]

Noel's report was advisory in nature, and was obviously tasked as a preliminary contingency plan; it frankly stated that the measures it suggested would need work "before we can even begin to appear serious" about elections. There is no evidence that the NJM was ever serious about the free and fair elections it had promised.

Despite the NJM *Manifesto* of 1973 which promised that political participation by all groups (even Gairy's GULP) would be allowed, once in power the NJM allowed no political opposition to organize. The Grenada National

[29] *CMB*, August-September 1979, pp.20-21.

[30] Document 2305/1003664: Minutes of NJM Central Committee Plenary, 19-23 July 1983.

[31] Document 8174: "Structure and preparation of Field Force for a General Election," Lloyd Noel, undated. Noel resigned as PRG attorney general in 1981, tried to start an independent newspaper, and was arrested. See also Document 11655: "Report to the P.B.: Situation in Jamaica as of 5/11/80," report by agent of Special Branch.

Party (GNP), which had been Gairy's main political rival and a one-time partner of the NJM in the People's Alliance, still existed under the leadership of Herbert Blaize (at this writing, the prime minister of a free Grenada), but public meetings of the GNP were broken up by organized NJM supporters, who acted despite the presence of police. Coard denied on PRG television that the meetings had been broken up by the Party; the people had just expressed their will, as was "their democratic right." This activity effectively nullified cosmetic reform measures such as the PRG's lifting of restrictions on public use of public address systems.[32]

The Zonal and Workers Councils, those people's assemblies which in replacing Parliament were supposed to represent a pure form of democracy, were little more than glorified "rap" sessions. This institution was praised by the PRG elite as an exercise in true democracy superior to the backward form of representative democracy. Because a PRG official was always present at these Councils, it was said, the government knew the will of all the people, all the time. The argument, of course, fails for two reasons: first, there was no accountability either through elections or popular recall; and second, at no time did the Party ever relinquish its claim to be the true interpreter of the ideology which *by definition* represented the general will.

Reports were made by the PRG officials—many of whom were not Party members—of the proceedings of these Councils; perhaps this was done primarily to carry the charade to the sub-elites, because there is no evidence that these reports were used in any way other than as an instrument to judge the mood in a particular parish. This information might be discussed at higher-level Party meetings, but one example serves to indicate how the leadership regarded this data: it was reported at a Political and Economic Bureau meeting that there was much discontent in the parish of St. Andrew's over the Party's plan for industrialization of this primarily agricultural region. Rather than consider that the genuine voice of the people had been heard, the disagreement was attributed to "the high degree of parochialism evident in that parish." Similarly, at the same meeting "the unfavorable mood of the masses to the Revolution" in the parish of St. David's was blamed on the failure of certain Party comrades to "develop" the area. As Arendt notes, the only thing that matters to totalitarians is consistency. In the NJM experience it was inconsistent, or perhaps unthinkable, that the people could simply disagree with the vanguard Party.[33]

Most of the time, it must be concluded, the people were disregarded. For example, an entire set of original Zonal Council reports from all parishes was ignored. These documents have no routing slips, no cover letters for

---

[32] For Coard's explanation see *CMB*, August-September 1979, pp.22-24.

[33] Document 6825: NJM Political and Economic Bureau minutes, 24 August 1983. For the consistency required by totalitarianism, see Arendt, pp.457-459.

someone's action or information, no marginal notes, nothing in the way of the usual bureaucratic evidence to indicate that they were read by anyone in the PRG; they were simply filed. Party discussion on the Zonal Councils was rare and was concerned only with control over these bodies; only locals who were invited by the Party could attend Zonal Council meetings, and they had to present their invitations at the door. One Party report indicates the NJM's attitude regarding issues which were potentially explosive, which could not be avoided, and which would certainly have been voted down if Grenada had been a true democracy; the Party recommended that discussions in the Zonal Councils regarding the PRG's efforts to curtail religious education would "have to be carefully engineered" so as to be presented as an issue of time rather than of religion:

The matter . . . need not be presented as an issue revolving around Religion. The issue can be that there simply is not enough time in the present time-table for all the ground the children have to cover . . . the time allocations worked out can be simply presented to the Zonal Councils . . . Communities would therefore be discussing *the curriculum* rather than the issue of religion in the schools.[34]

The PRG regarded the institution of a free and independent press in the same light as democratic ideals or political opposition; which is to say, they were not to be tolerated. It was known from open sources that the PRG was hostile to a press uncontrolled by the Party, and the archives confirm what was believed to be true—that the Party could scarcely have cared less about the "CIA connection" it had been shouting about, and simply did not believe in press freedom on its merits. Abuse of *Torchlight*, Grenada's only newspaper, began early. In May of 1979, barely six weeks after the NJM coup, two fires occurred on the island; one burned down a cottage inhabited by a madman, the other damaged a travel agency. Bishop took to the airwaves, and in a speech on Radio Free Grenada blamed the fires on a "CIA program" to destabilize the country; the CIA was also blamed for the bad press Grenada was receiving in the international media.

Torchlight, known for its conservative, anti-communist editorial stance, was singled out by Bishop as "a local agent of international reaction" which printed "classical CIA-planted anti-communist propaganda." In August, Bishop said at a press conference that the PRG was considering measures to ensure that the press behaved "in a free and responsible way." *Torchlight* was again singled out for printing "scurrilous" material "aimed at discrediting the Revolution," and for not representing the majority view. The NJM called on the Grenadian people to put *Torchlight* "under heavy, heavy manners"; the people "must be aware of the dangerous part which a lying

---

[34] Document 12467: "Religion and the Education System: Primary Schools," undated PRG report (but probably pre-1982). For the NJM's disdainful attitude toward the Zonal Councils, see Document 12436: "Zonal Councils on the Economy," parish reports, 25 February to 9 March 1983. See also Document 2324/100465: NJM Central Committee minutes, 23 and 28 September 1983.

newspaper can play against a progressive People's Government." The PRG took special exception to one issue which reported that the PRG was harassing the country's Rastafarian community.

On 13 October 1979 the paper was closed down for not representing the views of the majority of the Grenadian people, and on 26 October the PRG issued People's Law 81, which limited ownership by one Grenadian to no more than 4% of the capital of a newspaper. In other words, 25 partners were thus required to operate a newspaper. Announcing the closure in a radio broadcast, Defense Minister Hudson Austin declared that "those who don't realize there is a revolution will simply have to learn the hard way."[35]

That the closure of the country's only independent paper was not the will of the majority of Grenadian people is shown by a Special Branch (secret police) report on the unfavorable mass sentiment to the closure in the parishes of St. George's and St. Andrew's—parishes in which the majority of the Grenadian population resides:

Persons feel that the closure of the Torchlight is not in keeping with Government promise of Freedom of the Press. They feel that Grenadian Journalists are more muzzled today than in the past days. . . . Persons also criticized Government for limiting individual shares in the Torchlight, and said Government is dictating to people what to own or how much to own. . . . Some persons are of the opinion that the N.J.M. could never win an election, if they should continue in this manner.[36]

Four months later, the PRG silenced the only other medium of independent thought, *Catholic Focus*, the newsletter of the Roman Catholic diocese; in this case, the charge was that the journal had violated the law because it was printed on the presses of the banned *Torchlight*.

The intent behind People's Law 81, which required at least 25 owners for a newspaper, was obviously to dilute editorial opinion even if the requisite number of individuals could agree on the establishment and operation of the newspaper. It must have come as a surprise to the Party, then, when it was announced at a 12 June 1981 meeting of the Economic Bureau that an independent newspaper, the *Grenadian Voice*, had just gone on sale. This new paper, with 26 shareholders (including former Attorney General Lloyd Noel), was published within the strict letter of the law; in its first editorial, the paper stated that it did not support counterrevolution in any form, but rejected the idea that criticism of government was an act of destabilization, CIA or otherwise. The *Grenadian Voice* also called on the PRG to keep its promise of early and free elections. Bishop immediately recommended to

---

[35] The campaign against *Torchlight* is best documented by *CMB* issues for May, August-September, and October-November 1979. See also Maurice Bishop, *Selected Speeches, 1979-1981* (Havana, 1982).

[36] Document 5183: Special Branch report to Bishop on popular discontent toward *Torchlight* closure, 30 October 1979.

the Economic Bureau that the law be amended so that no newspaper could be published prior to the issuance of a PRG media policy; this was done on 18 June. The NJM announced that the 26 owners of the paper were CIA dupes and bourgeois exploiters who had been "exploiting both workers and the public for years."

As the paper prepared its second issue for publication, its publishing equipment was seized and three of its staff were arrested (including Lloyd Noel, who was to remain imprisoned until set free by U.S. forces). No PRG media policy was ever announced, and no opposition press emerged during the remaining life of the PRG. Bishop warned those that might attempt another "counterrevolutionary newspaper" that

This is a revolution, we live in a revolutionary Grenada, this is a revolutionary condition, and there is a revolutionary legality, and they will have to abide by the laws of the revolution.

When the revolution speaks, it must be heard. . . . The voice of the masses must be listened to, their rules must be obeyed. When the revolution orders, it must be obeyed. The revolution must be respected. . . . They are going to understand that counterrevolutionary activity will be met by revolutionary action . . . by revolutionary manners as the comrades say . . . Don't touch the revo.[37]

More to the point, Bishop specified how the Revolution generally viewed democratic freedoms in his confidential "Line of March for the Party" speech before a general meeting of the NJM. After assuring the membership that "we have hegemonic control on power," Bishop made it clear that only the Party decided how far freedoms could go:

Just consider, comrades, how laws are made in this country. Laws are made in this country when Cabinet agrees and I sign a document on behalf of Cabinet. And then that is what everybody in the country—like it or don't like it—has to follow. . . .

It is also important to note, comrades, that while we are in an alliance with sections of the bourgeoisie, they are not part of our dictatorship . . . because when they try to hold public meetings and we don't want that, the masses shut down the meeting. When we want to hold Zonal Councils and we don't want them there, we keep them out. When they want to put out [a] newspaper and we don't want that, we close it down. When they want freedom of expression to attack the Government or to link up with the CIA and we don't want that, we crush them and jail them. They are not part of the dictatorship. In fact, if the truth is told, they have been repressed by the dictatorship. They have lost some of the rights they used to have. . . . The point is that all rights are not for them, all freedoms are not for them . . . the majority will crush, oppress and repress the recalcitrant minority.[38]

The Police and Population Control

The Services

It is generally recognized by theorists of totalitarianism that, along with the traits of a single party and loss of political freedoms, the existence of a

---

[37] "Freedom of the Press and Imperialist Destabilization," in *Maurice Bishop Speaks*, pp.150-166.

[38] Document 12203: Bishop's "Line of March" speech, 13 September 1983.

political police is a requisite element of the totalitarian regime; this government organ is purely a party instrument to remove all opposition and stand guard against potential dissent through both calculated and random terror. The political police force is the means by which the party, in Maurice Bishop's words, "will crush, oppress and repress the recalcitrant minority." The concept is identified with the totalitarian state to such a degree that any deviation from the image of an omnipotent, ruthless, terroristic secret police quite rightly casts doubt on whether the state has achieved totalitarian status. It is in this area, that of the power and activities of the secret police, that the totalitarian label on the Grenadian experience begins to seem less appropriate.

Under the PRG there were three organizations with police powers. The regular police, numbering between 300 and 400, were charged primarily with conventional criminal work; their political duties were at most auxiliary in nature, and consisted of merely keeping the peace by an increased presence in a "problem parish," such as St. Andrew's. The police were armed by the PRA and took part in major military maneuvers, being tasked with population control in emergencies.

The role of the PRA as the "sword and shield" of the Party has already been discussed. It is clear that the PRA had primacy over any other organization as the "defender of the Revolution": from the earliest days of the NJM regime, the PRA was given the police powers of search, seizure and arrest; PRA troops protected both Bishop and Coard; the PRA provided guards for the prisons; and, under the Prison Act of 1980, all political prisoners (*not* criminals) were in the legal custody of the PRA. It is not surprising to find a PRA report of June 1979 recommending physical and procedural improvements to the existing prison system as the arrests of political prisoners increased in the early months of NJM rule. The PRA was also tasked by the Party with enforcing a monopoly on weapons throughout the country.[39]

"Special Branch" was Grenada's secret police, although perceiving any similarity between this organization and the Gestapo or Soviet security services requires a greatly stretched imagination. It was not terroristic, omnipotent or ruthless in its operations, just secret. First of all, Special Branch was tiny, even by Grenadian standards. Although there certainly was the opportunity (courtesy of East Germany) to create a larger, well-trained and technologically advanced security service, the NJM apparently thought that to increase the size of Special Branch would be an insult to the loyalty of the PRA. Consequently, a Special Branch personnel roster of July

---

[39] Document 8900: PRA report on prisons, 21 June 1979. See also Document 8901: Letter from Prison Commissioner to PRA chief General Hudson Austin, 7 July 1981. On the weapons monopoly—a recognized totalitarian trait—see Document 5046: Letter from Major Louison to NJM Central Committee, 10 May 1981. The PRA estimated that only 5 percent of the arms on the island were not under PRA or police control.

1980 lists only 18 people.[40] It is clear that the primary function of Special Branch was clandestine intelligence collection, which is but one of the recognized tasks of a full-service intelligence organization. Virtually all the Special Branch reports examined by the author are concerned only with surveillance, rumors, and illegal publications. No evidence was found of covert political action. Intelligence analysis was limited to individual political profiles. Counterintelligence was handled by the PRA. It is doubtful whether Special Branch agents even carried weapons. Any operation which involved direct or violent action, such as the campaign against the Rastafarians, was the exclusive domain of the PRA. If only for its lack of applied terror, Special Branch cannot be considered a totalitarian police.

Despite its limitations in size and function, Special Branch carried out a remarkable number and variety of clandestine operations. A permanent "watch list" was maintained on all possible "counters," including all journalists and all foreign diplomats; when U.S. Ambassador Sally Shelton visited Grenada in December 1979 her activities were monitored constantly, as well as those of persons having any contact with her. Surveillance was also conducted on other foreign nationals in Grenada and Grenadians returning from abroad; Special Branch took careful note of immigrants' political opinions of the PRG. Although Special Branch apparently had neither the manpower nor the tasking for penetration of the PRA officer corps, it did report on any hints of dissent within the PRA, militia, and PRG rank-and-file. Seditious conversations and suspicious gatherings were promptly reported. Mail was regularly intercepted. Persons reported to be involved in political activity not sanctioned by NJM were investigated. The Rastafarians as a group were labelled "lumpens," and were under constant surveillance.

All reports were sent directly to Bishop who, in addition to being prime minister and Party leader, was minister of national security. Any unauthorized publication received instant notice; Special Branch would report on the existence of a new publication, such as the *Grenadian Voice*, the NJM leadership would order it closed, and the PRA would carry out the order. Shortly after *Catholic Focus* was shut down in February 1980, a student newspaper appeared, the *Student Voice*. Special Branch identified the students involved and where it was published; it too was closed.[41]

---

[40] Document 6982: "List of Special Branch Personnel," 23 July 1980. Given the large number of surveillance targets, it is certain that Special Branch employed a large number of informants.

[41] Documents 5183, 5310, 7101, 8537: Various Special Branch reports. Document 7095: Surveillance report on U.S. Ambassador Sally Shelton.

The majority of Special Branch surveillance activity centered on the two sources of political dissent considered most dangerous to the Grenadian dictatorship of the proletariat, namely, the unions and churches. The attitude toward and the plans to control these groups will be examined later, but the Special Branch tasking in this regard is illuminating.

Every aspect of church activity in Grenada was subject to the cognizance of Special Branch. Clergymen were followed in their daily ministrations and watched even while at home: "We are watching the subject closely and will report on his activities, we have a man in the Rectory."[42] Special Branch agents went regularly to services, posing as faithful parishioners. Sermons were the object of careful attention, especially when they touched on political matters.

The reading was about the people selling what they had and offering the returns to the poor. While discussing this reading the priest said 'The Communists use this as a strong point to show the people that this is communism since from the beginning. But don't be fooled, the communists don't believe in God.' At that service were about 180 people.

The proceedings of religious seminars were monitored and lists of attendees provided to the PRG. At one such seminar, sponsored by the Caribbean Council of Churches,

. . . the nature of the discussions centered on the Detainees question and the involvement of School Children in the militia. The Churches decided to 'protest' against this. The CPE [the PRG's adult education program] was also openly criticized as the participants felt that this was the PRG's way of teaching Communist Ideology.

Special Branch also reported:

Although most of the Churches in Grenada are keeping [a] low profile, one Church, the Roman Catholic Church, seems to be spearheading a well planned campaign to incite the others to active opposition to the P.R.G. and the Revolution.[43]

Like the churches, the unions were expected by the NJM not to trouble themselves with politics—at least to the extent of questioning the NJM's regime. The Party's distress over the failure of the unions to remain apolitical was reflected in regular Special Branch infiltration of union meetings and workers' groups. The possibility of strikes was viewed by the NJM as especially dangerous; strikes not only hurt the economy but challenged the Party's role as the vanguard of the masses. A Special Branch report on plans for a farmers' strike, for example, named the leader and supporters of the "agitation" and included personal details such as past political affiliations. Persons calling for a strike in the teachers' union, unhappy because of low pay and government control of the curriculum, were identified by an agent who had infiltrated a union meeting. Similar infiltration and reporting

---

[42] Document 8877: Special Branch report on the Roman Catholic Church, 22 April 1982.
[43] Document 7133: Special Branch reports on Grenada's churches, classified Top Secret, 11 and 29 December 1980.

occurred at meetings of dockworkers, customs workers, revenue collectors, taxi drivers, and hospital workers. Union officials and supporters of the union position in salary disputes with the government were identified by name, categorized with a political profile and placed under surveillance if considered "reactionary" or "backward" enough or identified as having "Gairyite" or "lumpen" tendencies.[44]

Given this level of domestic surveillance activity, it is surprising that Special Branch conducted operations abroad as well. The security services of at least one neighboring island-state, St. Vincent, were penetrated by an agent working for the PRG; from one report on the regional political situation provided by Special Branch, it seems likely that agencies of other governments were also targets of Special Branch infiltration. It is clear that agents regularly went abroad, perhaps as tourists, to collect information on local politics and Grenadian emigre communities.[45]

Political Prisoners

Although wholesale imprisonment was used by the Party as one of the primary instruments of political repression, here again the evidence seems not to warrant granting the PRG the status of a totalitarian state.

Political prisoners made up the majority of the prison population under the PRG. In contrast to the Soviet Gulag, however, the government tried to keep criminal and political elements in the prisons separate. Political prisoners, called "detainees" by the regime to distinguish them from the criminal "prisoners," were treated the same as the convicted prisoners, in that work was compulsory for both. A "detainee," however, was a different legal being altogether. By law in the custody of the PRA, political prisoners had no right to legal assistance because they were undergoing temporary "preventative detention." The minister of national security—that is, Bishop in his capacity as prime minister—was authorized by People's Law 21/1979 to detain persons "in such place and under such conditions as the Minister may from time to time direct."[46] The law required that the government provide the "detainee" with orders stating the reasons for the detention within seven days of arrest, but this law was widely disregarded. While a convicted prisoner could earn remission of up to one third of the sentence for good behavior, this option was denied to "detainees." The law provided for the review of these political cases; a Preventative Detention Tribunal was established at which either criminal charges would be preferred or the

---

[44] Document 5562: Special Branch report on farmers' strike, 23 January 1981. Document 6168: Special Branch report on Teachers' Union meeting, 26 February 1981. Documents 6168, 6169: Special Branch reports on union activities, February-March 1981.

[45] Documents 5183, 7139: Special Branch reports on operations abroad.

[46] *CMB*, September 1981, p.16. People's Law (P.L.) 21/1979 was amended by P.L. 29/1981, "Preventative Detention Regulations," which gave the PRG broad powers over citizens' physical movements.

"detainee" would be released. Originally supposed to meet every two months, the Tribunal's required convening was changed to every six months; the Tribunal actually met only three times in 1979, once at the end of 1980, and never met again after that.

The Preventative Detention Tribunals actually released few prisoners. The prison population steadily increased until it reached nearly 400 by the end of 1981; this meant that about one of every 300 Grenadians was imprisoned. The number of prisoners was then reduced by half as the combined result of unfavorable foreign press reports, international pressure exerted by groups such as Amnesty International, and diplomatic efforts. Those prisoners that were released were forced to sign a "Certificate of Release from Detention" which amounted to a confession:

[I certify that] I had been detained in the interests of National Security . . . or in connection with matters and/or activities of a subversive and Counter Revolutionary nature. I further certify that since my detention on [date] I was not subjected to any form of torture or ill treatment in any way. . . .[47]

Released "detainees" were also required to sign a "Voluntary Declaration," promising not to engage in "counterrevolutionary or subversive activities" and that

I shall always endeavour to cooperate with the People's Revolutionary Government in [the] future and that I will promptly report to the appropriate authority any person, group of persons or organisation, here or abroad, who attempt to or who are actually involved and/or engaged in any form of Counter Revolutionary or subversive activities. . . .[48]

In order to control the activities of released prisoners, they were required to report periodically to a local police station; any violation of their "voluntary declaration" would result in re-imprisonment.[49]

Political prisoners were often left in prison, without benefit of trial or even formal charges, for months or even years. U.S. forces released about 100 political prisoners, some of whom had been in prison for over four years. The PRG called political prisoners dangerous counterrevolutionaries, or even terrorists, although the evidence indicates that they were just persons considered potentially critical of the regime; their imprisonment was primarily to remove them from society, not so much to discover conspiracies as to prevent them. In March 1980 one "detainee" petitioned Bishop to review his case; he had been picked up the previous November and hadn't been asked a single question in over four months. Another political prisoner who had been arrested in July 1981 wrote to Bishop in March 1982, politely

---

[47] Document 8980: Detainees' file.
[48] Ibid.
[49] Documents 8318, 8871, 8900, 8901: Prison Service records, October 1979 to April 1982. Document 6776: Ministry of Interior prison report for 1981-1982.

requesting the interrogation on his "counterrevolutionary activities" that the PRA had promised him at the time of his arrest; he, too, had never been questioned during his eight-month incarceration.[50]

Despite the gag rule on the released prisoners, reports of mistreatment and even torture reached the foreign media. According to testimony before the OAS Inter-American Commission on Human Rights by Dr. Stanley Cyrus, a professor at Howard University who interviewed former "detainees" and who would himself be imprisoned in Grenada as a CIA agent, the PRG concocted a countercoup in November 1979, the so-called "DeRaveniere plot," in order to round up individuals unsympathetic to the PRG who might know how to handle weapons. It is known that the imprisoned included many former Royal Grenada Police and military members. According to the testimony presented by Dr. Cyrus, men were tortured by Special Branch by beatings with a hammer or rifle-butt on the forehead, knee, elbow, foot, and abdomen. Other forms of torture included being forced to stand for hours with arms straight out to the side, not being allowed to relieve oneself, and the placing in the nostril of a lighted cigarette. Prisoners who were injured or injured themselves were not given medical treatment. One Rastafarian leader who was arrested after calling for free elections at "Rasta" meetings was beaten with the butt of a gun and then underwent a mock execution; later the man was wounded by gunfire, allegedly "shot while trying to escape." Another man was shot in the leg and spent a year in prison with the bullet still embedded in his leg.

In fact, real shootings for staged escapes may have been part of the solution for problem "detainees"; though the evidence is not conclusive, it is certainly suggestive. A PRA report on prison security improvements concluded with:

The present situation is unsatisfactory. *If inviting escape is to be part of the eliminating process* then this must be carefully planned.[51]

Bishop may have been too honest when, at a Jamaican news conference, he defended the practice of detaining political opponents without charges:

In any situation of a revolution, there must be counterrevolution, a necessary period of dislocation. The choice is between a firing squad, pretended shoot-outs in the hills, pretended accidents, or detention.[52]

Besides the two men mentioned by Dr. Cyrus, at least one other prisoner suffered from the "shot while trying to escape" syndrome. In May of 1981, WCBS-TV of New York reported on Antoine Langdon, a Grenadian-born

---

[50] Documents 5183, 2151/103291: Petitions to Bishop from political prisoners, 24 March 1980 and 19 March 1982.

[51] Document 8900: PRA report on improving prison security, 21 June 1979; emphasis added.

[52] Quoted in Stafford Earle, *The Grenada Massacre* (St. Ann, Jamaica: Earle Publishers, 1983), p.33.

Brooklyn shop owner who was arrested while vacationing in Grenada for having sold anti-PRG literature in his Brooklyn business. Friends reported that Langdon was "shot while trying to escape"—in the chest. PRG prison and medical documents confirm the existence and location of the wound. A Party history of the "detainee situation" after the March 1979 coup acknowledges that three detainees were "killed in Military action" in the period 1979-1981, but the report is silent on details.[53]

Likewise, there is no conclusive proof that torture was a policy of the PRG, though it is clear from the documents that it occurred. One document, which recommended the release of several non-dangerous prisoners because of expense and over-crowding, notes that one man who had been scheduled for release was kept because he complained in writing of being tortured at Fort Rupert (PRA headquarters): "it was decided to stay his release in the interests of unfavorable propaganda." The report goes on to say that this man could be released at a later time, restricted to Grenada for one year and then deported to his native St. Vincent; "this might serve to counter any desire on his part to publicise the treatment *he received at the Fort.*" The only case of mistreatment that was certainly known to the leadership was that of an Eddie Richardson, who was beaten up by his PRA guards during a transport in view of private citizens. The report of this event concludes that action must be taken against the guards because of the public exposure and previous bad press:

In view of the fact that only up to recently, the P.R.G. was the target of a bitter and concentrated attack from the Mass Media charging and associating it with the infliction of torture to Detainees, however unfounded, malicious and mischevious, [this beating,] which took place in the presence of a few members of the Public, must be seriously discouraged and condemned.[54]

Though it is likely that the NJM leadership knew of and condoned the mistreatment, torture, and perhaps even murder of political prisoners, there is so far a lack of conclusive evidence that these totalitarian actions were part of systematic Party policy. For the present, one can at most conclude that the police system could have evolved, with outside assistance, into a more terroristic, powerful, and therefore more totalitarian entity.

Fraternal Assistance

Thanks to the help planned and provided by the Soviet Union and its network of client states, the police and prison system of the PRG was indeed targeted for significant organizational, operational, and ideological improvements. The archives indicate three major areas and sources for these improvements: Cuba (police organization), Vietnam (reeducation program), and the Soviet bloc (technological improvements).

---

[53] Document 8901: Prison medical reports on detainees, 2 June 1980 and 13 October 1980.
[54] Document 7139: "Report on the Ill Treatment of Eddie Richardson," 29 March 1982. Document 6804: Report to Bishop on detainees situation, 29 September 1981; emphasis added.

It is now known that Cuba not only trained members of the Grenadian police force in criminological methods, but that the training extended to ideological instruction. The acting commissioner of police assured Bishop that a six-month course attended by 20 Grenadians would include

. . . a Basic Course in the Principle of Marxism, Lenin, and Engels, as a matter of fact quite a number of hours of study would be spent on those subjects.[55]

This evidence alone could mean merely that the police were receiving ideological training like everyone else in Grenadian society, and would not necessarily expand their scope of activity from their established primary function of criminal prosecution. A top secret Cuban report on the Grenada Police Service, however, indicates that the intention was to make the police more ideological in function. In apparent response to a PRG request to improve the entire security system, Cuba recommended a complete reorganization and professionalization of the regular police force. The report first recommends replacing any present members of the force who had ties with the previous regime with "revolutionary cadres," who would then provide the ideological basis for the overall professionalization of the police corps. The force was to be imbued with "revolutionary faithfulness and discipline." Cuba also recommended the establishment of a political officer structure within the police force. Whether Cuba's recommendations were carried out beyond the ideological content of the police course is not known, but there exists a fragment of a letter from the PRG's Ministry of Interior (to whom only the police and prisons service reported, among all the security services) which requests Cuban assistance in the design and construction of a "Detention and Interrogation Centre" specifically for political prisoners. This is further evidence that perhaps the role of the regular police was being expanded, with Cuban assistance, to make it the predominant security service in political matters.[56]

Part of the plethora of assistance provided to the PRG from the Soviet bloc was in the form of security equipment. The German Democratic Republic (GDR) specializes in security assistance to Soviet client states such as Cuba and Nicaragua; the GDR accordingly agreed to outfit the security services of Grenada and, perhaps in a related area, was also upgrading the island's telephone system. The USSR was directly petitioned in a PRA equipment request to provide a variety of security equipment:

---

[55] Document 9240: Letter from Acting Commissioner of Police to Bishop on Cuban police course, 5 August 1980.

[56] Document 6903: Top Secret Cuban Report on the Grenada Police Service, mid-1980. Document 8312: Ministry of Interior letter fragment to Cuba, date unknown.

... micro-cassette recorders (for secret recordings) ... mini cameras and accessories (for secret operative photography) ... video tape and T.V. system ... mini microphone and accessories for bugging purposes. ...[57]

The equipment, although ordered through PRA channels, could have been intended for an expanded political police. In any case, the equipment would have provided the NJM with an enhanced capability, whether through the instrument of the PRA, Special Branch or the Police Service, to monitor and thereby control the population.[58]

The greatest evidence for a growing totalitarian tendency on the part of the police and prison system of the PRG is in the area of reeducation, recognized by Bertram Wolfe, Robert Jay Lifton, and Jeane Kirkpatrick as characteristic of such a system. In early 1981 the Party decided to seek assistance in the reeducation of recalcitrant dissidents and so-called "lumpen" elements such as the Rastafarians; the decision to embark on a reeducation program was probably made much earlier. In May 1981 the PRG made a formal request to Vietnam to provide PRA chief Hudson Austin, scheduled for a visit to Vietnam in June, presentations on various techniques of warfare and also

Counter-intelligence techniques ... Techniques of dealing with counter-revolutionaries especially in the area of reeducation ... Methods of dealing with lumpen elements.[59]

The request was granted, and Austin spent two weeks in Vietnam observing, among other things, the "struggle against reactionary and social enemies." Austin reported to the Party leadership that one day of his tour was devoted to visiting a reeducation camp in operation since 13 April 1975, in which were imprisoned 350 ex-RVN officers and government officials, as well as Christian and Buddhist priests—all of which were referred to in the report as "the criminals." Overall, Austin was impressed with Vietnam's efforts in the reeducation field:

The solid effects of the U.S. culture and morals is still left in the south. The Party has done a lot since the revolution to rehabilitate many of the anti-social elements breeded by the vulgar Yankee environment.[60]

While Austin was in Vietnam developing his appreciation for Vietnamese techniques in "rehabilitating" its "anti-social elements," the Party was addressing the "Rasta problem." The Rastafarians were long considered a potentially permanent symbol of defiance to the NJM's attempts to re-order society because of their apolitical, undisciplined, marijuana-filled mystical lifestyle.

---

[57] Document 2309: Appendix II to PRA draft request for Soviet equipment deliveries for 1983-1985, undated.

[58] Document 12241: Ministry of Industry letter to GDR Ministry of Foreign Trade, 24 July 1981. See also the letter from the Cuban Ministry of the Interior regarding GDR security equipment, in Uri Ra'anan, et. al., editors, *Hydra of Carnage* (Lexington, Mass.: Lexington Books, 1986), pp.382-383.

[59] Letter from PRG ambassador in Cuba to Vietnamese ambassador in Ra'anan, *Hydra of Carnage*, pp.373-374.

[60] Document 6112: General Austin's report of PRG delegation to Vietnam, 4-17 June 1981.

The Rastafarians were becoming more of a problem as the Party tried to impose greater controls on the independently-minded Rasta community. When PRA forces tried to destroy the marijuana crop in the hills, for example, they were fired upon; reportedly several PRA soldiers died in such gun battles. Party members suggested several solutions to handle the estimated 600 to 2,000 Rastas in Grenada, including making living in the hills illegal or incarcerating the lot on prison farms. Coard's wife Phyllis (a hard-liner herself) argued for a "selective pickup" of 50 or so of the top Rasta leadership. With the beginnings of a reeducation program already in motion, Bishop directed the PRA to

. . . prepare a programme for the rastas who will be picked up—wake up time, eat time, books, films, pacifying music, etc.—a rigid programme.[61]

Within a month the PRA and the Prison Service had jointly created a draft program for reeducation, no doubt based on the Vietnamese experience. This Party-controlled program was to be imposed on any persons requiring rehabilitation.

RE-EDUCATION PROGRAMME
PHASE ONE (1) Six (6) MONTHS

0530—Awake with Music FORWARD MARCH. Loud enough to awake all.

0600—Sanitation in todays scientific World. A Voice Lecture on Sanitation. (Simple) on Tape.

0700—The meaning of March 13th Revolution (3mts).

0800—*This Re-education School* (Appropriate Music) total silence, must be demanded from the beginning. your attitude during this period will assist the authorities to determine how many years you will be required to stay here and your meal time
(1) What is Re-education in a Revolution.
(Tape)
(2) The Revolution demands of all citizens.

0900—Breakfast.
Persons misconducting themselves during the quiet period, will be given one (1) hour Physical productive work. . . . All form of eating must be regulated and from start of this programme eating must be at the sitting position for the period stipulated.

0930—Tape, the purpose of Food and Digestion.

0945—Tape, mans physical fitness.

1000—Physical exercise to be rigidly supervised. . . .

1100—Productive work—School Supervisor and Farm Officer to carry out rigidly and on time.

1400—Lunch. Music during Lunch—Mozart
local Calypso on the Revo or Folk song on the Revo progressive Reggae.

1500—News Prime Minister's speeches.
Tape the patriotic Grenadian

1600—Productive work with special instruction. . . .

1900—Supper

---

[61] NJM Central Committee minutes of 6 and 14 June 1981, in Romerstein and Ledeen, document 97.

2030——The meaning of March 13th Revolution.
       Quiet time soft—progressive Poetry.

2100——FORWARD MARCH—Lights out, Silence.

It is not known whether this strict regimen, with its aim of inculcating revolutionary ideals into political dissidents, was ever implemented; the NJM probably did not have the time to take it beyond a planning stage. It is certain, however, that the Party intended to implement a reeducation program: Vietnam subsequently agreed to train 20 Grenadians in the "reeducation of anti-social and counter-revolutionary elements."[62]

---

[62] Document 8505: Minutes of meeting between PRA and Prison Service, 14 July 1981. Cuban letter to PRG ambassador in Havana, undated, in Ra'anan, *Hydra of Carnage*, pp.374-375.

2. The Party and the Masses

As described by Hannah Arendt, a totalitarian system attempts to replace all previously existing relationships between individuals with the single relationship permitted in the new order—that between the individual and the party. In Arendt's terms, the liquidation of all classes is the means by which individuals become atomized and isolated. The party, already masquerading as a state, will continue the charade as the media, a sports club, or even the Church, but the end remains the same: no loyalties are permitted, except to the party.

This section will examine the attitude of the NJM toward the traditional social forces of Grenada and the efforts of the Party to control the interaction of these forces and replace them with the Party-individual relationship. Particular emphasis will be given to agitation and propaganda (agit/prop) activities, religion and the churches, the PRG media, education and youth, the unions, and the role of culture.

Agitation and Propaganda

The goal of "mass mobilization," which in totalitarian parlance means developing the loyalty of the population, was sought by the NJM through a two-pronged approach. From the top, Bishop and other Party leaders would exhort the masses to greater vigilance against the enemies of the Revolution; from the bottom the Party, in the guise of "mass organizations," would carry out activities designed to develop mass loyalty to the Party.

Each of the six parishes had a Party group assigned to coordinate the mass mobilization activities of the organizations which targeted the various social groups of the parish: workers, youth, women, etc. There were also solidarity groups such as the Soviet-Grenadian, Cuban-Grenadian, and Nicaraguan-Grenadian Friendship Societies. The following specific objectives of the Parish Coordinating Boards (PCB) are distilled from their workplans for 1982:

To raise the consciousness of the masses.

To raise the PCB members' ideological level.

To increase parish participation in the militia and adult education.

To coordinate all Party work in the parish.

To raise funds for the Party [annual target was $10,000 to $20,000, depending on the parish].

To help organize cooperatives, mobilize the masses for PRG work days and rallies, and to encourage the masses to deposit with the People's Bank.

To improve propaganda within the parish.[63]

The PCBs reported to the Party's Organizing Committee, which was headed by Coard. One set of minutes illustrates the activities of the organizations for which the PCBs were responsible. All mass organizations were tasked with lining the streets and cheering in the villages for the arrival of Mozambique's communist leader Samora Machel in May 1982; children from the Young Pioneers in St. Andrew's parish were assigned to meet Machel at the airport and present flowers, and unions were to carry banners in honor of his visit. In addition, buntings, posters and pamphlets were to be printed and distributed. Similar activities were planned for the visit of any fraternal comrade or the visit of a Soviet or Cuban ship; May Day, Lenin's birthday, and commemorations of Ché Guevara and Sandino; days celebrated in solidarity with the FSLN, the FDR, SWAPO, the PLO, POLISARIO, and Angola; holidays celebrating events and heroes of the "Grenadian Revolution"; and so forth. A great deal of monetary and organizational resources were devoted to these feast days, more numerous than the high holy days of all the combined religions of the world. Large numbers of people were attracted because of the free food, the entertainment provided (which always had a political message), a chance to see celebrities both imported and domestic, and because they would get the day off from work if they attended; transportation was courtesy of the government. The mass organizations also mobilized ordinary citizens for free trips abroad for the purposes of indoctrination provided by, for example, the Cuban Institute for Friendship Among the Peoples (ICAP).[64]

While the ideological consciousness of masses was being manipulated by the Party in the guise of popular groups, the NJM leadership was simultaneously working to mobilize the population in support of the Party through speeches, appearances at rallies, and broadcasts on Party-controlled radio. Despite the allegedly "non-aligned" stance of the PRG, the interpretations of the history of "imperialism," "colonialism," "Zionism," and "racism" presented in public announcements were always in accord with standard Soviet propaganda. Claims made by these declarations included, for example, that the U.S. blew up the *Maine* in order to colonize Cuba; that the United States waited out both World Wars in order to see who would win; and that the Soviet Union came to the aid of the Afghan Revolution because of the CIA. The CIA was blamed for all events embarrassing to the Party, from the emer-

---

[63] Document 6869: Parish Coordinating Board workplans for 1982.
[64] Document 12201: Minutes of Organizing Committee, 17 May 1982. Document 2024/00162: Pocket calendar of NJM member Derek Allard, 1983.

gence of a medium of dissent such as the *Grenadian Voice* to a demand by foreign oil companies to pay overdue fuel bills. References to counterrevolutionary and subversive elements, an invasion of CIA mercenaries headed by Gairy, or related CIA-backed destabilization efforts appeared in virtually every speech or radio address made by Bishop; the masses were told to inform on the least suspicion of subversion. In order to feed anti-CIA hysteria, the Party enlisted the assistance of Philip Agee and John Stockwell, both of whom addressed public rallies, mass organizations, and the military.[65] Party members were advised how to "beat back the rumors" which the CIA was alleged to be supporting in Grenada, such as the Cuban and Soviet use of the international airport, the planned curtailing of emigration, a war on the Church, the rounding up of the Rastas:

Get out to the masses daily, tell them the rumours are nonsense . . . Explain to the masses how the CIA pushes rumours . . . Tell the masses clearly that anyone who pushes these rumours is helping the CIA to bring down the Revolution . . . Tell the masses we must look at who is pushing the rumours gleefully to hurt the PRG and send their names into the security forces.[66]

It is not the purpose of this paper to determine whether the PRG had genuine cause to fear CIA operations against the regime; that inquiry will require the declassification of certain CIA documents. One may speculate, however, that the campaign to unify the populace against the counterrevolutionary/CIA/Gairyite subversives hoping to turn Grenada into a squalid prison of U.S. imperialism had its origin not in authentic concern on the part of the top NJM elite but rather in the classic political technique of unifying the masses in order to divert their attention from the failures or intentions of the leadership. The letters to Bishop from political prisoners who had been held for long periods without charges or interrogation regarding their alleged CIA employment have already been mentioned. Another piece of evidence exists which suggests that the Party was not genuinely fearful of the CIA threat. The fire that burned down a tourist cottage occupied by a mental patient was publicly attributed by Bishop to the CIA plot to destroy Grenada's tourist trade; this incident precipitated the usual vitriolic speeches and radio warnings. A police report to the leadership indicates, however, that the PRG was fully aware the madman himself had set the fire.[67]

---

[65] *Maurice Bishop Speaks*, especially pp.157-165. Documents 5800, 6913, 10639, and 11760 relate to Agee and Stockwell's visits. In return they were well treated: Agee was able to travel in West Germany on a Grenadian passport, and Stockwell's request to live in Grenada was approved.

[66] Document 9731: "Beat Back the Rumours," NJM directive to membership, undated.

[67] *Selected Speeches*, p.18. *Maurice Bishop Speaks*, pp.103-104. Document 12476: Police report of 15 May 1979.

The PRG Media

Our people are firmly taking control of their newspapers, their radio and TV. Our people will never again be controlled by the media.

—Maurice Bishop, August 1982

The complete monopoly of mass communications as a means of re-channelling society and even individual thought along the lines of the totalitarian party's ideology has been described by Friedrich and Brzezinski, George Kennan, and Hannah Arendt. The efficient elimination of any potential opposition press by the New Jewel Movement has already been examined. What follows is a discussion of the activities of the official PRG press and broadcast media, and their use as a Party instrument for mass mobilization.

The Party itself had eight publications; its primary propaganda instrument was the newspaper *New Jewel*. This organ had been in existence since the formation of the Party in 1973 and had a weekly circulation between 1,000 and 4,000, depending on paper shortages. The self-assigned task of the paper was "to lift the political and ideological level of the masses" by drawing "lessons from and inform[ing] our people on the progress of popular struggles around the world"; the *New Jewel* also purported

To consciously push and educate the masses of the need for greater world peace and security and other internationalist objectives [by] constantly exposing the war-mongering and anti-people policies of imperialism. . . .[68]

The *New Jewel*, one of the island's two biggest legal newspapers, provided the Grenadian people with a "progressive" view of the outside world modeled entirely on the official position of the Soviet Union. One issue from September 1983 is a typical example. Gus Hall, a "noted author" and a "leading American intellectual," is quoted as stating that the Korean aircraft shot down by the USSR was definitely on a spy mission; significantly, Gus Hall is not identified to the Grenadian populace as the leader of the American Communist Party. In the same issue is an extremely favorable article on the life of Lenin. The editorial committee of the paper told the employees of *New Jewel* what to write and how to write it:

Greater effort should be made on the part of the comrades to write news in an ideological way—to interpret news with a political slant; even sports articles. Every article should help to raise the political consciousness by the way in which it is written. And, the style should be more agitational.[69]

The evidence is that this was the Party's media policy in general, and applied to a far larger compass than the Party paper. Except for the Government Information Service, the PRG's official news agency, the rest of the legal media organizations in the country were nominally independent

---

[68] Document 6869: "Draft Workplan of the *New Jewel*'s Editorial Committee—1982."

[69] Document 11736: Minutes of *New Jewel* Editorial Committee meeting, 8 August 1981. See also Document 11621: *New Jewel*, 17 September 1983, pp.3, 8.

agencies. In reality, however, all reported to the PRG's "umbrella" media agency, the aptly-named State Propaganda Committee (SPC), which itself was no more than an arm of the Party's Propaganda Department. The SPC consisted of four agencies: Television Free Grenada (TFG), Radio Free Grenada (RFG), the Government Information Service (GIS), and the *Free West Indian* (FWI). The function of the SPC was to orchestrate, in its own words, a "planned propaganda offensive" when called upon by the Party. When assigned to respond to foreign criticism of Grenada's Cuban ties, for example, or when the Party wished to highlight its democratic charade of presenting the annual budget to the population, the SPC coordinated the propaganda campaign and tasked each of the media agencies with specific assignments.[70]

In order to communicate the proper ideological perspective to the masses, media personnel first underwent a security check prior to their employment, and were thereafter required to study the works of Marx and Lenin. As in any government agency, even the hint of dissent was not allowed; one RFG information officer was dismissed after joking about "Bishop and his boys." The Party had a purely pragmatic view of the normative role of the press.[71] As Bishop told an assembly of media workers,

The role of the patriotic media must be to help in the tasks of mobilizing and organizing the people around the constructive programs the revolution is putting forward.[72]

In other words, the role of the media was to plug the Party line. Bishop went on to say that media skills and technology "must serve the revolution," that the media are in the "front lines in the defense of the Revolution," and that the media must spread the word that there is a price counterrevolutionaries will have to pay—loss of their rights. Bishop concluded his speech with the curious words, "Long Live Responsible Journalism!"

Beyond the duties of the Party Propaganda Department and the State Propaganda Committee, the amount of interest and the attention to detail given by the Party elite toward ensuring that journalism met their standards of responsibility is impressive. A top Party leader such as Bishop, Coard or Austin had to check the week's issue of *Free West Indian* before it hit the streets. RFG programming schedules were submitted for approval to Bishop, who made changes in titles of programs, inserted programs on

---

[70] Document 6448: State Propaganda Committee meeting, 15 March 1983. See also Seabury and Douglass, *The Grenada Papers* (San Fransisco: Institute for Contemporary Studies, 1984), Document III-4, Propaganda Workplan for 1983.

[71] Document 10635: Radio Free Grenada letter, 20 July 1981. For the perspective required of the media, see Document 1292/100283: Political and Economic Bureau minutes, 3 August 1983.

[72] Document 2223/100244: Bishop speech to Media Workers' Association, 11 July 1981.

PRG projects such as the Young Pioneers, or deleted religious programming. Coard's interest in the ideological content of RFG extended to suggesting that it play only "progressive" music, including rock and calypso, drawn from an exclusively "progressive" 200-record library.[73]

The network of "fraternal" socialist states assisted the NJM in maintaining these propaganda instruments. Cuba provided, for example, a 50-kilowatt transmitter, which made RFG one of the most powerful radio stations in the Caribbean region. Cuba also supplied training for PRG media photographers, graphic artists, cartoonists, sound and film technicians, and newspaper staff. East Germany furnished two-month crash courses in journalism, while Romania and the Soviet Union offered four and five year scholarships so that Grenada need never be without "responsible journalists." East Germany also trained technicians for RFG; it appears likely that the GDR was to help establish two more radio stations, according to the report from PRG Ambassador Jacobs on his meeting with the GDR State Committee for Sound Broadcasting:

There followed a wide-ranging discussion about the *role of radio in the resocialization process*. Comrade Fischer expressed the view that RFG was doing a very good job. . . .[74]

The Soviet Union maintained a TASS office in its embassy in St. George's in order to supply well-written, ideologically sound material to Grenadian media. With a constant Marxist-Leninist slant in its reporting, for example, *Free West Indian* was considered by many foreigners, and no doubt many Grenadians, to be the Party journal. The NJM reciprocated the international assistance in this particular area by speaking against the "total information monopoly by the imperialist world" led, of course, by the U.S. media. Bishop pledged support for the "struggle to establish a New International Information Order" which would promote peace, disarmament, and detente, and which aimed at diminishing the information imperialism of non-progressive countries.[75]

The price paid for total control of the media is widespread disbelief. One significant example of the evidence that the NJM suffered from a real credibility problem, despite the Party's monopoly on the instruments of information, comes from Party cadre reports of early 1983. Despite the

[73] Documents 6495 and 11695: Economic Bureau minutes, 28 August 1981 and 28 April 1981. Document 8921: Proposed RFG schedule with Bishop's handwritten amendments, undated.
[74] Document 8538: PRG Ambassador Jacobs' report on his meeting with the GDR State Committee for Sound Broadcasting, 19 May 1983; emphasis added.
[75] Document 10583: PRG Press Secretary Don Rojas memo to Bishop, 10 February 1983. Document 5855: TASS releases on KAL 007 incident, September 1983. Document 2223/100244: Bishop's speech to Grenadian Media Workers' Association, 11 July 1981, and Bishop's speech to the First Conference of Caribbean Journalists, St. George's, 17 April 1982.

massive campaign to convince the population that the U.S. CIA threat had reached the point of imminent invasion, the field reports from each parish stated that 50% to 75% of the populace did not believe the PRG warnings of invasion.[76]

Education and Youth

Who Control the Minds of the people Have State Power.

—NJM Party Slogan, 1983

As Jeane Kirkpatrick observes, totalitarian regimes place great emphasis on the country's youth in the process of creating the new society promised by the ideology. Children and youth are less likely to be irrevocably "corrupted" by the outmoded attitudes of the previous, "backward" culture; they can be molded into untainted "new men" and thereby gladly take their places in the new order. From this supply of human silly-putty will also come the future leaders of the party. The ideological training comes from two sources, schools and extracurricular groups, both naturally under party control. Such is the totalitarian party's attitude toward the political development of youth, and such was the view of the NJM.

The philosophical position of the NJM with respect to education is best expressed by a PRG report on the Community School Day Program (CSDP), the Party's effort to combine education with production by requiring selected schools to grow crops. Referring to the "New Revolutionary Educational System,"

The stated objectives of the CSDP reflect the primary concerns [of the PRG] as it seeks to project the new Educational Thrust. The fundamental issues have to do with the intention of the People's Revolutionary Government to ensure that a new man, be he student or worker, farmer or peasant, be created for the demands of the new society which is being created. *The community and the School are basic factors in the process of creating both the new individual and the new society.*[77]

The PRG Ministry of Education, which concerned itself primarily with the standardization of the curriculum in the schools, was the instrument of the Party's Education Committee, the chairman of which was the deputy prime minister, Bernard Coard. Not just concerned with school curricula, this committee also oversaw the "ideological and political influence" of the adult literacy program, the island's cultural activities, even the showing of films in the cinemas. The Party recognized the importance of controlling the flow of ideas as much as possible; at an NJM general meeting a Leninist slogan was introduced between the discussion on making the education

---

[76] Document 10485: Party cadre reports to Organizing Committee, 28 March 1983.

[77] Document 10091: "Community School Day Program," undated PRG report; emphasis added. See also Bishop's "Education is Production Too!" speech in *Maurice Bishop Speaks*, pp.217-226. In the *Communist Manifesto*, Marx and Engels advocated combining education and industrial production.

44

minister a Central Committee member and a directive to the Young Pioneers to step up their ideological work. That slogan was: "Who Control the Minds of the people Have State Power."[78]

There were two major obstacles to controlling young people's minds in the schools: "reactionary" principals and teachers, and the absence of "political and patriotic education" due to the lack of a standardized curriculum. The problem of a "politically backward" school leadership was easily handled; twenty "right wing" principals were ousted in favor of twenty "democratic and progressive replacements." Fifteen of the twenty replaced had headed schools run by churches, eight of these by the Roman Catholic Church—identified as "leading the tactical offensive of the denominations" in opposing a standardized curriculum. The Central Committee recommended to the Politburo that the road to a politicized classroom was

> ... *total state ownership and control* of all educational institutions and [then] to revolutionise the content to reflect a patriotic, revolutionary and scientific outlook.[79]

In one case, the PRG was able to nationalize a Roman Catholic school, St. Mark's, by declaring it dilapidated and replacing it with a state-owned structure. In another case, a Methodist school, Wesley College, was simply declared to be state-owned. The church school boards were told that the PRG planned "to establish the hegemony of the State in education": NJM's Central Committee committed itself in July 1983 to the eventual nationalization of all church schools. In May of 1983 it was decided by the Party that all students in all Grenada's schools would receive political education disguised as "civics" or "social studies" courses, beginning in September. The beginning of that academic year, soon to be interrupted by the invasion, also brought the requirement in all schools that the school day begin with the national anthem, and end with the Party song "Forward March."[80]

The drive to fill the schools with "progressive" teachers required a PRG crash program, the Ministry of Education's National Inservice Teacher's Program (NISTEP). After the coordinator of the program voiced her concern that the PRG was being too hasty—742 of the 1100 primary and secondary teachers were described as unqualified—the NJM Central Committee

---

[78] Document 12475: Education Committee minutes, 9 August 1983. Document 2386: Agenda for NJM General Meeting, 12 October 1983. The slogan is also in Document 12601: Diary of NJM Member Andre McQueen, date illegible.

[79] Document 9203: "Education—Sport—Culture; Review and Perspectives," report of NJM Central Committee Plenary, July 1983, classified Confidential.

[80] Document 2305: Resolutions of NJM Central Committee Plenary, 18-23 July 1983. Document 2292/100288: Organizing Committee minutes, 9 May 1983. Document 5779: Jacqueline Creft's letter to Bishop, 8 September 1983; Creft, Minister of Education and Culture (as well as Bishop's mistress and mother of his son Vladimir), recommended changing the anthem and the flag which she said were "anachronistic, express bourgeois nationalist values and idealistic sentiments"—something the Coards might have suggested.

announced that twelve Soviet secondary teachers would arrive in 1983-1984 to assist the school system. Soviet assistance to the PRG educational program is also evident in the English-language Soviet textbooks found in Grenada: engineering, chemistry, geometry, physics, and political science textbooks were provided by the Soviet Union, and negotiations were ongoing for more texts on politics and international relations.[81]

Students in the schools were not only exposed to an increasingly politicized environment, but found themselves engaged in the form of "socialist competition" called "emulation" by Party leaders. "Emulation," not surprisingly a feature of both Party and military, was introduced into the schools "to raise the *collective* level of consciousness and production"; Stakhanovite-like performers in ideological work and on the schools farms were praised, for

. . . they will increase our production, teach and inspire others and produce yet greater harvests in the future years. That is the whole point of emulation, Comrades, it is not a static recognition, it pushes our process forward, it is the very motor of our advance. It *challenges* and *motivates* us at every juncture.[82]

Besides the political training being developed by the Party in the school system, thousands of children were mobilized in the quasi-military political organizations already known to countless Soviet, East European, and Cuban youngsters; these were the Young Pioneers. By early 1982 the Party claimed a Pioneer membership of 8,000 and planned to increase this to 15,000. Through Pioneer camps, social activities, military and political training, the Party aimed to develop a large, loyal cadre of Grenadian youth. The Young Pioneer workplan for 1982 included the following objectives:

To creatively raise the anti-imperialist consciousness of the pioneers and to step up the involvement of children in building the Revolution through mass activities. . . . To recruit and raise the political consciousness of pioneer guides. . . . To establish relations with other Pioneer organisations. . . .[83]

Children were recruited to the Young Pioneers through a Party-coordinated effort to attract them with sports, tours to historic sites of the "Revolution," cultural activities such as Youth Festivals and calypso competitions, rallies and marches on days of solidarity with Angola and Vietnam, dances, and raffles; the media assisted with a recruiting blitz using TV and radio promotions and the printing of the movement's monthly, the *Pioneer Voice*. Pioneer groups would hold political discussions and debates under the direction of Pioneer Guides, young adults who received regular political

[81] Document 11783: NISTEP Coordinator's report to Bishop, undated. Document 9203: NJM Central Committee Plenary report on education, July 1983. Documents 10761, 10762, 10769, 10771, 11593, 11594, 12194: Soviet textbooks. See also Document 9901: PRG Embassy in Moscow report on negotiations with USSR publisher Mezhdunarodnaya Kniga, 7 June 1983.

[82] Document 5842: Bishop speech at National Emulation Night, 29 October 1981.

[83] Document 6869: "National Work Plan for NJM Young Pioneer Movement" for 1982.

indoctrination. At Pioneer camps hundreds of children would wear Cuban- and Bulgarian-supplied uniforms, participate in marching drills, sing revolutionary songs, and receive rudimentary weapons training. Pioneers would be mobilized to do "voluntary work" on Sunday mornings in lieu of going to church. The movement sponsored an essay and poem competition; the topic assigned was "What I as a child can do to help build the Revolution." By indoctrinating all the island's children, the Party planned to transform Grenadian society in accordance with its Marxist-Leninist ideology: the goal of the Party was clearly identified as the "[m]obilisation of all children to partake in sports, culture, and educational activities undertaken by the Pioneer Movement."[84]

The Party ran a similar organization for teenagers and young adults. The National Youth Organization (NYO) claimed a membership of 7,700, and used the same methods as the Pioneers for recruiting: sports, cultural activities, rallies, community work, and media agit/prop. Like the Pioneers, the NYO ran military-style youth camps, the closing ceremonies of which ended with the singing of the "anti-imperialist anthem 'Forward March Against Imperialism.' " There was a greater NYO emphasis on political indoctrination, however; NYO was structured on the same lines as the NJM, with a Central Committee and various departments. The NYO reported to the NJM's Organizing Committee, headed by Coard. Moreover, all members were required to attend seminars and classes taught by NJM members (including Bishop himself) on subjects such as Marxist analysis of class, the "class content of the 13 March Revolution," historical materialism, and "Organisational Principles of the Revolutionary Vanguard." At these training sessions NYO members learned that the Party expected Grenadian youth to be in the forefront of transforming the country:

The building of the new society requires . . . the development of new relations between people and the upbringing of the new man. . . . The NYO would definitely and determinedly . . . develop and promote a rich progressive culture which would be a vehicle for the spiritual liberation of our people. The old backward psychology, values and attitudes of our people would definitely act as brakes on the further development of our revolution. . . . *This must be wiped out and the youth must take positive steps in promoting revolutionary culture.*[85]

This discussion of the NJM perspective on education would not be complete without at least brief mention of the adult literacy program, known as the Center for Popular Education (CPE). Like similar Cuban and Nicaraguan campaigns, the goal of CPE was to increase literacy so that adults could be indoctrinated in the objectives of the Party. There is no doubt that large numbers of adults, perhaps over half of Grenada's adult

---

[84] Document 10357: GIS release on Pioneer camp, 4 September 1981. Document 10406: NYO report on Pioneers, July 1982. See also *CMB*, January-February 1981, p.20.

[85] Document 5056: "NYO 1981 Draft Program"; emphasis added. Document 6869: NYO 1982 Workplan. See also Document 10357: GIS release on NYO camp, 7 September 1981; Document 6822: NJM Organizing Committee minutes, 19 October 1981.

population, received literacy training, although Bishop's claim that in one year illiteracy had been virtually wiped out in Grenada was certainly exaggerated (Castro made the same claim in 1960). The ideological slant of CPE was ensured by the fact that Cuba provided both the texts and many of the instructors. CPE publications echoed the same pro-communist, anti-U.S. stance of all other PRG and Party publications. CPE was one element in the overall orchestration of a society's educational processes and institutions toward the totalitarian goal of creating a new man and new society.[86]

The Unions

Since its formation, our Party has tried to organize the people of Grenada. We have given priority to the organization of the working class through the unions.

—Maurice Bishop, 1977[87]

A totalitarian party will extend its domination over the nation's unions for the same reasons that any nominally independent body must be controlled: education of the masses along party lines, espionage on non-party elements, and an established organization to neutralize anti-party elements.

Union control under the PRG was the domain of the NJM's Workers' Committee, which made reports directly to Bishop. One such report on the history of the Grenadian working class reveals that the NJM's objectives with respect to the workers and the unions were identical with the Party's objectives for Grenadian society as a whole. The Workers' Committee stated that the Party required of the working class

political support, participation in programs and activities of the revolution, lifting of productive levels and discipline, building of an anti-imperialist/socialist consciousness.[88]

To this end, the report continues, the Party must first maintain "organised control over the working class" through the unions, workers' committees and other mass organizations; secondly, the Party must also maintain "ideological control over the working class" through workers' education, films, rallies, visits by the political leadership and trade unionists from fraternal countries, and "progressive literature and propaganda."

"Organised control over the working class," step one in the two-pronged Party plan, began early. Vincent Noel, NJM Central Committee and Politburo member as well as a PRG minister, was at the time of the March 1979

---

[86] Document 10170: Bishop letter to Castro on CPE texts, 11 December 1981. Document 12449: Ministry of Education report, 2 March 1981. Document 2292/100291: Politburo minutes, 22 June 1983. See also *Maurice Bishop Speaks*, pp.120-123, 296.

[87] Interview with Cuban weekly *Bohemia*, 19 August 1977, reprinted in *Maurice Bishop Speaks*, pp.16-23.

[88] Document 5054: NJM Workers' Committee report to Bishop on the history and situation of the working class, undated.

coup the head of one union, vice-president of another, and vice-president of the trade union council. Despite accusations of conflict of interest, when the PRG was formed Noel retained his union positions, his Party rank, and also became a government minister. Then followed a Party campaign for the eventual takeover of the unions. By March 1980 Noel was able to report to W. Richard Jacobs, then PRG Ambassador to Cuba, that real progress was being made on taking control of the unions and countering the "pro-imperialist elements":

We have been able to have elected our entire slate, exactly to final plan, of progressive and center-left elements as officers of the Trade Union Council. Chalky [John Ventour, NJM Politburo member] is the General Secretary; I am 2nd Vice-President. Things look very good for the future . . . we will be able to defeat backward and reactionary ideas in the trade union movement locally, and replace them with sound working class ideology.[89]

Thereafter, Fitzroy Bain, NJM Central Committee member, became the president of the country's agricultural union. Bishop was proud that most of the union leadership in place at the time of the coup had been "thrown into the dustbin of history." By the end of 1981 Party hegemony over the island's union activities was complete. The Documents indicate the level of micro-management the Party exercised in its concern over labor; the unions had to submit new constitutions for approval, and Bishop himself read and amended drafts so as to limit union autonomy. In one case, for example, Bishop changed "General Meetings of the Union shall be at least once every month" to read "twice per year."[90]

Because the Party viewed the unions as instruments by which the workers could be organized and therefore controlled, it aimed at unionizing all of Grenada's workers. This process was well served by a PRG law that made all government workers members of the Public Workers Union; as more of Grenada's economy became nationalized, more workers came under Party influence. The nationalization process also assisted Party ideological objectives; government workers were required by law to attend weekly socialism classes. The methods by which workers were recruited into Party-controlled unions were described by Stanley Roberts, an official of a non-government controlled union, in a letter to the Caribbean Congress of Labor:

. . . representatives of Governmental Oriented Union[s] intimidate the workers, forcing them to sign up membership cards, tak[ing] a "poll" without proper Free Trade Union practices . . . Generally speaking, the Free Trade Union Movement is going through a phase of undemo-cratic actions, where workers are intimidated, and in more recent times almost daily . . .

---

[89] Document 6913: Vincent Noel's letter to Ambassador Jacobs in Cuba, 27 March 1980.

[90] Documents 5387, 5388, 8956: Draft union constitutions with Bishop's handwritten notes and amendments (quote is from Document 8956). See also Bishop's speech of 18 November 1981, in *Maurice Bishop Speaks*, p.230.

rumour[s] have been going around that shortly Brother Stuart and myself are going to be picked up, because we are indirectly in a plot through our Trade Union activities to overthrow the People's Revolutionary Government.[91]

Roberts' concern about the independence of the unions and their publications caused Bishop to denounce him in June 1981 as a corrupt, opportunist CIA stooge. The following month Roberts was taken into custody as a political "detainee." Probably due to criticism over these heavy-handed tactics, the Party shifted to a more subtle recruiting campaign similar to those used by the NYO and Young Pioneers: sports, cultural and social activities, pressure from workers' Party cells, the "emulation" program, plus a media blitz on the benefits of union membership (although Special Branch continued its surveillance of workers potentially hostile to the Party, as described in a previous section). In July 1981 Bishop claimed that 85% of the island's workers had been unionized.[92]

A unionized worker was subject to a great deal of ideological attention from the Party. The shop stewards were assigned to distribute "progressive literature" in the workplaces, such as *Granma, Moscow News, Northern Neighbors* (the Canadian version of *Soviet Life*), and the NJM's own *Workers Voice*. The shop stewards also reported to the union on the ideological composition of the workers, who were categorized as "close to Party," "center," "right wing," and "backward reactionary." Weekly political indoctrination was compulsory for government employees and was "encouraged" for independent, private sector shops by approaching the "individual capitalists" and applying pressure. (One factory resisted but agreed to hold the classes every two weeks.) Eventually, "socialism classes" were held at almost 80 different workplaces in the country: the docks, factories, banks, utility companies, schools, and the hospital. Run by union Party cadres (the Farmers' Union identified a "Political Commissar" for the job), the classes utilized historical materials, such as Lenin's "Should Revolutionaries Work in Reactionary Trade Unions," Stalin's "On Problems of Organizational Leadership," and Soviet-provided literature on the international workers' movement. The workers were exhorted to increase production, to show solidarity with workers of other socialist countries by participating in May Day rallies and other activities, to read the "progressive literature," and to help recruit more workers into the movement.

---

[91] Documents 8119 and 8120: Reports by Stanley Roberts to the Caribbean Congress of Labor on trade union activities for October and November 1979.

[92] Bishop's speech of 19 June 1981, *Maurice Bishop Speaks*, p.158. "List of Persons in Detention As of 1st January 1982," document 6 in Romerstein and Ledeen. Document 5369: Workers' Committee workplan for 1983. Bishop interview of 12 July 1981 with *Granma Weekly Review*, reprinted in *Maurice Bishop Speaks*, p.185. Document 10480: Supplementary Workers' Committee report to Politburo, 3 November 1982.

They were taught Marxist analyses of class and history. The workers were told that the international airport project was "the single most important activity of the revolution and is a symbol of a break with the backward and dependent past."[93]

Dissent was often voiced at these indoctrination sessions, which indicates that the Party's efforts to accomplish the ideological uplifting of the working class had not translated into the widespread fear characteristic of a genuine totalitarian state. The workers complained about the nationalization of private property, the lack of elections, the anti-U.S. rhetoric, the number of foreigners in the country, the PRG praise of the Soviet Union despite the news of Poland and Afghanistan, and so forth. Predictably, the Party characterized these opinions not as genuine working class views, but rather as indicative of the low ideological development of the people who held them. The Workers' Committee reported to the NJM Central Committee in July 1983,

The level of political consciousness of the working class at this time is generally low but increasing. One a scale of 0 to 10 it is about 2.0. This represents an increase during the period under review of about 0.65. . . .

Similar evaluations were made on the "patriotic consciousness of the working class" and "Trade Union consciousness." (It is perhaps symptomatic of the ideological arrogance of totalitarians that consciousness can be quantified to the point of registering a 6.5% increase over a six-month period.) Even the considerable fraternal assistance provided by the Soviet Union—visits by Soviet "trade unionists," tours of the USSR by Grenadian trade unionists (including ten-month training sessions), projectors, public address systems and films—was not giving Grenadian workers the correct, Party-approved political perspective. The Party identified one primary source as the cause for its disappointment regarding working class consciousness—the churches. Religion was more than a handy scapegoat for the failure of the workers to line up solidly with the Party; indeed, religion was seen by the NJM as the major obstacle to the new order.[94]

---

[93] Document 2109/00119: Workers' class syllabus, undated. Document 6960: "List of workplaces—Socialism classes," undated. Document 5369: Workers' Committee workplan for 1983, undated. Document 6869: Farmers' Union workplan for 1982, undated. Document 8213: Workers' Committee report to NJM Central Committee Plenary, 13-19 July 1983. Document 5843: Party memo to union members on study materials for 13 February 1982. Document 12470: Shop Steward reporting form for workers' political views, undated.

[94] For workers' dissent, see Document 8160: Report on Workers' Education classes for 29 April to 6 May 1983; Document 11690: Report on Workers' Education classes for August 1983; and Document 8213, ibid. For Soviet assistance, see Document 10481: Workers' Committee report on visit of Comrade Pichigin, 10 September 1982; Document 9923: Report from PRG Embassy in Moscow, 3 June 1983; Document 12470: Meeting of airport construction workers' union, 29 June 1983. For the blaming of religion, see Document 11690, and Document 11624: Workers' Committee report to Bishop, undated.

Religion as Enemy

The Government of the criminal dictator Eric M. Gairy has been overthrown . . . A Revolutionary Government has been formed, all religious rights and freedoms are now restored . . . .

—*Radio Free Grenada, 13 March 1979*

Amongst the working class, persistent ideological backwardness and economism exist . . . we are witnessing widespread and ever expanding activities of the Church.

—*NJM Central Committee, September 1983*

Totalitarians deny God's existence for intellectual reasons; God was invented by immature man, they say, to explain what could not be explained before the dawn of scientific knowledge. The totalitarian ideology provides the scientific solution to all of man's questions, so God is rendered superfluous. Yet the totalitarian attitude toward religion goes beyond mere denial of superstition; it is downright hostile. Totalitarian opposition to religion is grounded in the fact that the ideology is a formula for absolute power, and allegiance to another threatens the legitimacy of the totalitarian elite. Belief in God, moreover, denies the omniscience of the ideology and the omnipotence of its driving force—the dialectic, history, race, whatever. On a more practical level, believers do not participate in the mass enthusiasm that the totalitarian state cultivates; as one prominent Latin American politician put it, if a man believes in God he will not "lose himself" in earthly patriotism.[95] Moreover, the church will often be identified by the totalitarian regime as the center of all opposition in the state. Lenin recognized the religious threat to totalitarian ideology and required as early as 1905 that the Party struggle against such "obscurantism." Going beyond Marx's "opiate of the people" dictum, Lenin expressed the totalitarian's contempt for and hatred of religion in a letter to Maxim Gorki:

Every religious idea, every idea of God, even flirting with the idea of God, is unutterable vileness . . . vileness of the most dangerous kind . . . Every defense or justification of the idea of God, even the most refined, the best intentioned, is a justification of reaction.[96]

Churchmen, representatives of the corrupt society being transformed by the new leadership, suffer special abuse at the hands of totalitarians. Clergy are a familiar sight in the Gulag, as they were in the Nazi camps, and countless believers have been martyred for their faith. At the same time, totalitarian leaders proclaim the complete freedom of religious worship—this mostly for foreign consumption. In no way does a totalitarian state admit that it fears the power of religion.

A similar case may be made for Grenada under the New Jewel Movement, although there was not the degree of religious persecution one finds in fully totalitarian societies. Despite the PRG's claim that religion in Grenada had

---

[95] Juan Jose Arevalo, *Anti-Kommunism in Latin America* (New York: Lyle Stuart, 1963), pp.128-129.

[96] Quoted in Robert Conquest, *V.I. Lenin* (New York: Viking Press, 1972), p.55.

never known more freedom than under its benevolent rule, all the churches in Grenada were subject to government interference, and the Party made it clear to its members that religion was the primary obstacle to effecting the transformation of society and the creation of the "new Grenadian."

It appears that members of the NJM, the vanguard of the new society, were expected not to subscribe to bourgeois superstition. Although no documents were found actually prohibiting Party members from going to church or believing in God, an NJM training document reveals that the required course of study for a Party member was designed to eliminate any "lingering belief in God." So that the children of Party members would not be tainted with religion, attendance at church-run schools was prohibited.[97]

Although Marxism-Leninism dictates a war on religion, and despite the history of communist persecution of churches in the Soviet Union, Eastern Europe, and Asia, it seems that the NJM initially hoped that the churches would passively go with the program. But by late 1979 the churches had made known to the regime their concerns about political prisoners, free elections, freedom of the press, and religious liberty. Thereafter the churches were identified in Party documents as agents of reaction and imperialism. Of initial concern was the loyalty the churches were thought to command with the youth of Grenada, the "future of the Revo." A December 1979 document of the Party's youth cadre reported that, because the Catholic Church "controls backward and idealistic youth," it was necessary to create a Religion Committee in order to oppose the Church's influence. The Party hoped to lure youth away from religion by indoctrination in historical materialism through NYO and Young Pioneer groups; by using Sundays as "NYO Day" for community work and social events; and by dismantling the religious education programs in Grenada's schools.[98]

The Party's efforts to remove "every idea of God" from education through curriculum standardization, PRG takeover of religious schools, and the removal of "backward" teachers have been presented in a previous section. The one document which best reveals the attitude of the Party to religious education, and to religion in general, is a PRG report on the situation in primary schools.[99] Starting with the morning assembly, at which prayers are said, the report attacks every manifestation of religion in the schools. The report states that religion must be controlled, if not indeed abolished, because

---

[97] Document 11733: Party Indoctrination Proposals, undated. Document 2109/00123: NJM Central Committee minutes, 14 September 1983. Compare with "A Permanent Standing Commitment to Freedom of Worship and Religion," in *Maurice Bishop Speaks*, pp.60-69.

[98] Document 12187: NYO Central Committee report to NJM Central Committee, December 1979. Document 6822: NJM Organizing Committee minutes, 2 November 1981.

[99] Document 12467: "Religion and the Education System: Primary Schools," undated PRG paper (probably pre-1982).

[it] has the effect of extracting the child from the real world from the moment he/she enters school—extracting the child, in particular, from the context of the Revolution.

As an interim measure before the eventual extinction of religion in schools, the report recommends concentrating religious education in the early morning; by making it early and optional, attendance would be discouraged. The conclusion of the paper reveals a typical totalitarian attitude toward an opposing ideology, namely, that it is totalitarian in nature:

The most devastating and pervasive trend [in Grenada's schools] is the Christian syndrome into which young minds are being locked . . . The Ministry of Education and the Government of this country will have to take positive measures to help the poverty of mind that dogmatic, evangelical religions perpetuate . . . God's will is used to stultify and bludgeon young minds. Christian dogmatism is bred through ignorance, it thrives on fear, and the greatest victims are the young, malleable minds . . . history has shown that no other force has done more to cripple the minds of people, especially the young. . . .

In fact, the language used at meetings of the Party leadership when referring to religion and the activities of the churches indicates that the Party considered religion almost as an ideological equal, with many of the Leninist attributes the Party was trying to develop in itself. A Party applicant study group in January 1982 discussed "clear evidence of a recent step up in [the] political offensive of the churches against the revolution"; the "clear evidence" against the churches consisted of praying for political prisoners and discussion of the atheistic character of communism. Likewise, at about the same time the Party's Central Committee concluded that

the relation of class forces show that the major enemy of the revolution is still imperialism which has the support of a section of the bourgeoisie manifested mainly through the Catholic Church.

In other words, the Church represented to the Party the greatest domestic threat to the Revolution.[100]

The rhetoric against religion continued throughout the life of the PRG. At the important July 1983 plenary of the Party Central Committee, when the Party was trying to figure out why the country was falling apart, why the Grenadian people were not supportive of the Revolution, and why the Party was in danger of falling from power, one Party member after another rose to speak to point out the causes for failure. As a rule, the Party blamed itself for not being Leninist enough; it blamed the masses for their backwardness and bourgeois attitudes; and it blamed the Church for everything—from asserting and building its influence with youth, women, peasants, and the masses in general, to spreading counterrevolutionary propaganda. All the Party comrades agreed that something would have to be done about the

---

[100] Document 10536: NJM Central Committee Plenary minutes, 30 December 1981 to 12 February 1982. Document 6869: Party Applicant Study Group Resolution, 12 January 1982.

churches, but at no time were concrete proposals made. Similar sentiments against the churches, accompanied by the same vague solutions, were made in September 1983, very late in the regime.[101]

In fact, little direct action was ever taken against the churches. Despite the rhetoric, which was certainly totalitarian in intent, acts of violence and terror such as occurred in Soviet Russia in the 1920s against clergy, congregations, and churches were absent in Grenada. At the same time, what actions were taken by the Party clearly established its hostile intent with respect to religion.

One area of great Party concern, nearly as important as the campaign for a religion-free youth, was the religious quarantine established around the "defense of the Revolution," the PRA. The military's political training also included regular anti-church indoctrination. Soldiers were told that joining or belonging to a church was counterrevolutionary—certainly not a career-enhancing move. PRA counterintelligence kept lists of "soldiers having strong sentiments to the church" (a separate list was drawn up for Rastafarians in the military), and soldiers were forbidden to have religious literature in their possession. The military, the section of Grenadian society over which the Party exercised the greatest control, was not allowed to partake of religious celebrations; for this reason they were even confined to barracks for the two weeks surrounding Christmas.[102]

Party interest in preventing the dissemination of "religious propaganda" extended to the top of the leadership. The personal efforts of Maurice Bishop to curtail religious programming on Radio Free Grenada have been detailed in a previous section. That this was a Party-wide concern is indicated by a Central Committee resolution that, because too many religious programs were being broadcast, all foreign-oriented programs were to be scrapped.[103]

Also covered in a previous section, that on secret police activities, was the high degree of surveillance of the churches conducted by Special Branch. Agents monitored sermons for political content, reported on everything from concern for political prisoners—considered to be an anti-PRG sentiment—to the number of parishioners attending and the quality of their clothing. Clerics were regularly followed in the course of their daily ministrations, and Special Branch even penetrated a Roman Catholic rectory in order to watch

---

[101] Document 2305/100364 and Document 11786: NJM Central Committee Plenary, 13-19 July 1983. Document 2109/00123: NJM Central Committee "Extraordinary Meetings," 14 and 17 September 1983.

[102] Document 2297: PRA Training Report, 14 March 1983. Document 8503: PRA Counterintelligence report, June 1981. Document 2219: Logistics Base Command Log for March-October 1983. See also Seabury and McDougall, document IV-1, Top Secret report to Bishop on Catholic Church publications, 11 February 1980.

[103] Document 2505/100364: NJM Central Committee Plenary minutes, 18-23 July 1983.

the priests there. It appears that all surveillance activity commenced with the closing of the journal *Catholic Focus* in February 1980—which itself seems to have been spurred by the Party's realization in late 1979 that the churches were not going to remain quiet on political matters.[104]

Apparently there was enough concern over religion's threat to the Revolution for Cuban intelligence to step in and conduct its own independent monitoring activities; later, Cuban surveillance was conducted in cooperation with Special Branch operations. Cuba provided intelligence on the strength and influence of each church in Grenada, and identified those "progressive" clergymen—that is, those favorable to liberation theology— who might be recruited to support the programs of the PRG; these clerics would receive a trip to Havana to continue their studies on the "achievements of the Revolution." (Subsequent Special Branch reports reflected the Cuban contribution; the reports were much more complete regarding identification of "dangerous priests," analysis was expanded, and specific recommendations were made.)[105]

On one such report Bishop added an item to the list of Special Branch recommendations which indicates the direction the Party was taking, with foreign assistance, on the issue of religion. In addition to measures which included increased cooperation with Cuba, contacts with liberation theologians, and increased political indoctrination countrywide, Bishop added "Start progressive church (talk with Nicar . . + Cuban)."[106] It was obviously hoped to create a benign church favorable to the Revolution, perhaps on the model of the Soviet "Living Church" of the 1920s, or collaborative churches in the PRC, Eastern Europe, or Nicaragua today. Vietnam also contributed to the NJM's knowledge of how to handle religion: at a January 1983 meeting of the Non-Aligned Movement in Managua, the Vietnamese delegation met with the PRG's representatives and "shared experiences on how they tackled the difficult question of the Catholic Church." Such "experiences" are well known; they involve reeducation camps.[107]

The available evidence, then, is somewhat contradictory. On the one hand, the Party was obviously hostile to religion, both in principle and as shown by its actions to decrease religious influence everywhere possible. The

---

[104] The earliest known Special Branch report of operations directed against the churches is from 18 February 1980; Roman Catholic sermons were being monitored and priests were followed after Bishop's "Commitment to Freedom of Worship" radio address (*Maurice Bishop Speaks*, pp.60-69).

[105] Seabury and McDougall, document IV-2: Cuban Report on Grenada's Churches, 14 October 1982. Romerstein and Ledeen, documents 3 through 5: Special Branch reports.

[106] Romerstein and Ledeen, document 5.

[107] Document 2293/100298: Report of Extraordinary meeting of Latin American and Caribbean Non-Aligned Movement countries in Managua, 10-14 January 1983. For an inside look at Vietnam's "reeducation" program, see Doan Van Toai and David Chanoff, *The Vietnamese Gulag* (New York: Simon and Schuster, 1986).

Party evidently intended to expand its counter-religious activity, probably to include the eventual replacement of Grenada's existing Roman Catholic Church—identified as the greatest obstacle to the Revolution—with one based on liberation theology and supportive of the regime. The possibility of forced reeducation of clergy was apparently considered.

On the other hand, despite the extent of surveillance and harassment of Grenada's churches, there was a marked absence of "revolutionary violence" directed against religion; in fact, to someone familiar with the history of communist desecrations and atrocities, particularly in the Soviet Union and in China, the Grenadian situation seems almost benign. Services were monitored, but congregations were not rounded up for imprisonment. Clergymen were followed, and some were warned about their "counterrevolutionary" activities; but none were subjected to violence, nor apparently were any clerics jailed at any time. In fact, one Ministry of Interior report shows that ministers of all denominations were allowed to come to the prisons to provide services and Bible classes to the imprisoned. In general, the Party exhibited uncommon restraint in its activities against religion; its attitude toward religion was totalitarian in intent rather than in action. This restraint on behavior certainly did not reflect any benevolence felt for religion and was probably due to a combination of causes, including intense international scrutiny and the PRG's efforts to appear a non-totalitarian government. Another important factor was the traditionally high degree of Grenadian piety; the Cubans estimated that over 80% of the population suffered from some form of religious belief. The Party knew that a direct assault on religion would require a Soviet-style "Red Terror" that would be impossible to conceal, given the international attention directed to the PRG.

It must be remembered, however, that the NJM was in power for only four and one-half years. Given more time to consolidate its power over Grenadian society—with the "fraternal assistance" of Cuba, Vietnam, North Korea, and the Soviet Union—and given the great potential for extreme means provided by its totalitarian ideology, one must conclude that the churches in Grenada would eventually have been subject to complete control, if not destruction, at the hands of the Party.

Implementing Culture

Culture is the ideological reflection of the politics and economics of a society.

—PRG editorial, 1981[108]

Contrary to popular opinion, the most significant contribution of Jeane Kirkpatrick to the study of totalitarianism is not her observation that

---

[108] Document 10081: PRG newspaper, *Free West Indian*, 23 February 1981.

right-wing, authoritarian states sometimes evolve toward democratic reform while left-wing, totalitarian states never do; this distinction was recognized as early as 1940 by Franz Borkenau. Kirkpatrick's major contribution is her emphasis on totalitarianism as a counterculture transforming itself into culture. The totalitarian ideology not only aims at changing the face of government, education, the economy, indeed, the entire physical structure of society; it seeks to wipe away all vestiges of existing, backward, corrupt society in its drive to create the "new man." This totalism of intended change represents a counterculture which, after it supplants the decadent culture, itself becomes the society's only culture; every aspect of society, from the fine arts to nursery rhymes, is thereby placed in its proper, revolutionary context.[109]

Turning its Marxist-Leninist counterculture into Grenadian culture was precisely what the Party planned to do. Its monopoly over the country's mass media enabled the Party to present a constant barrage of ideologically correct music, drama, and dance to the people. Pioneers learned in their youth camps songs and chants which, unlike songs sung by innocent children around the world, carried specific political meanings. Children as young as five or six would, for example, march about singing denunciations of imperialism or President Reagan. Adults, whether in the armed forces or in the unions, were also taught revolutionary songs, such as:

The AK speaking spanish and Reagan he can't understand it,
Tell Ronald Reagan the AK speaking spanish.
The AK speaking spanish and Reagan he too manish.
. . . You can't stop the Grenada Revo.,
—Reagan AK in your ass,
—Reagan mortar in your ass,
—Reagan A.A. in your ass. . . .[110]

Most of the Revolution's poetry, song, and theater seems to have been the product of Party member Chris DeRiggs. Described by the Party as the "people's poet," this West Indian combination of Mayakovsky and Maxim Gorki was a regular feature at Zonal Council meetings, at which he would attempt to drive the audience (one hesitates to call the attendees "participants") into an anti-U.S. frenzy with impassioned readings of his poetry, which as a rule evoked folk religious or voodoo themes along with its political message.

They come, an army of the bewitched
The haunted, the depraved souls
Servants of President Neutron
the most wicked and evil vampire

---

[109] Kirkpatrick, pp.108-116.
[110] Document 2012/00042: "Revolutionary Songs and Chants," undated.

the world has ever known
No. 1 hater of humanity
And eater of little babies.

They are here, they come to do battle
To take our land and make a hell out of it . . .[111]

For younger audiences, DeRiggs wrote plays about idealistic young people who, against great odds, overcome evil represented by foreigners or Gairy-like figures.

Youth, as always, are considered crucial to any totalitarian transformation of society; hence the great lengths the Party went to in order to indoctrinate them. Besides placing the country's educational system into a revolutionary context, the Party initiated cultural programs and social events to give the young people's extracurricular activity a political character via the Young Pioneers and NYO. These activities included songfests, steel band competitions, and "limbo" dance contests, all run by Party personnel and therefore intended to be ideologically sound.

An important area of Party concern regarding youth culture was sports, and the language used by the Party in this area indicates that more was at stake than winning teams. In discussing the planned National Institute of Sports, which would have coordinated all sports activity in the country, the Party's Economic Bureau stated that the purpose of the Institute was to ensure that political tactics were used "as a basis for the development of sports." The Institute was to have a propaganda department to "inform the people of strides made by the Revolution in the coordination of sports." The NYO reported to the NJM Politburo its progress in "capturing the leadership" of the existing sports associations which were characterized by "reactionary and backward" attitudes; such a process was being implemented, the NYO said, by "democratic infiltration." Apparently the process was not being completed quickly enough: at the July 1983 Plenary the Central Committee complained that ". . . sports are still being conducted without firm political control and direction and has not taken on a mass character."[112]

Similar Leninist language was used regarding performing artists. A PRG troupe of actors, dancers and singers toured England in 1982, performing mainly for West Indian communities. The majority of the production, which apparently was very successful, consisted of song and dance numbers which proclaimed the Party line, namely, that Grenada's entire history had been directed toward the March 1979 Revolution. On the troupe's return to Grenada, the Culture Depart-

---

[111] "Is Freedom We Making": The New Democracy in Grenada (St. George's: PRG, 1981), pp.6-7. See also Document 10489: DeRiggs revolutionary play.

[112] Document 5547: NJM Economic Bureau minutes, 3 June 1983. Document 9940: National Institute of Sports proposal, undated. Document 8532: NYO report to NJM Politburo on sports associations, 29 December 1982. Document 9225: NJM Central Committee resolutions from plenary 13-19 July 1983.

ment of the Ministry of Education reported on individual performers; unlike artists in the Western tradition, the performers were judged on whether they were "receptive to teaching and discipline," if they had "good levels of patriotism" and were "willing to learn about the Revolution." One artist was judged "strong[ly] individualistic . . . politically, a strong vacillator . . . should be monitored closely and attempts made by the cultural department to retrain him." Yet another had a "religious outlook . . . needs guidance."[113]

As stated by an official of the Cultural Department, "Culture is warfare—continuous fighting." Such is the attitude of the totalitarian state, until the time when its redemptive counterculture has finally replaced the old, corrupt culture. The same official wrote:

. . . we can transform the Society . . . using the totality of culture as an effective planner of our sociological development in today's world, thus providing voluntary National Security, moral guidance, and the development and progress of a revolutionary culture advancement in Grenada. . . .[114]

The importance of culture in the transformation of Grenada is highlighted by the Party's plans to create a separate and powerful Ministry of Culture.[115] Citing "the need to transform culture into a mass movement involving mass organisations, schools, and the society as a whole," the Party planned to place all of the island's cultural, sports, and social events under its control so that the population would develop a "revolutionary cultural consciousness." The Party saw no intrinsic value in cultural activities themselves; culture's worth was solely dependent on its revolutionary context. For example, the Party's attitude toward traditional folk dance is illuminating:

Traditional Dances: The main purpose of this type of activity is to transform and utilize the very strong cultural undercurrent to elaborate on and reinforce the program and policies of the Revolution.[116]

The heights of absurdity reached by the totalitarian attitude toward culture is reflected by the Party's views on Caribbean steel pan music:

Pan is a child of struggle born of the dialectical tensions between an inherently oppressive system (superstructure) and an oppressed people's need [to] liberate their creativity.[117]

Indeed, totalitarian culture makes one want to reach for one's gun.

As expected, fraternal assistance in this area was forthcoming. The web of agreements between Grenada and the Soviet bloc included cultural exchanges; through "friendship societies" both sides agreed to promote

---

[113] Document 10371: Report of Activities on Cultural Group tour of England, 19 April-18 May 1982.

[114] Document 10371: "Culture and its Technology as a Science," PRG report, August 1980.

[115] Documents 11727 and 2291/100275: Draft 1983-1985 Plan for Culture, 20 April 1982. One document on Adult Education (CPE) used the unfortunate term "Cultural Revolution" in referring to PRG policy; see Document 10580.

[116] Document 11727: Draft 1983-1985 Plan for Culture, 20 April 1982.

[117] Ibid.

the brighter aspects of each other's culture. Cuba in particular provided revolutionary literature, videotapes, and exchanges of cultural groups. On a more practical level Cuba was also helping the PRG build a Museum of the Revolution and a National Cultural Center, both crucial to the Party's intention to transform Grenadian culture. To assist the Party's sports monopoly, North Korea agreed to provide materials and funding for a stadium that could seat 15,000—well over a tenth of the population.[118]

As in most of the areas discussed in this monograph, it is an open question whether the NJM, given more time, would have implemented its own form of culture in Grenada. The totalitarian intent to transform society completely was clearly there. One suspects that at least part of the reason for practical restraint on the part of the NJM was the shadow of the United States, which even the Party must have realized would not countenance a Caribbean version of the typical totalitarian solution to cultural problems, namely, a "cultural revolution." In any case, the Party failed to implement its culture; no greater testimony to that failure exists than the outpouring of gratitude exhibited by the people when the president of the United States visited Grenada in February 1986. Despite over four years of DeRiggs poems and dialectical steel pan, the Grenadian people praised the president as, in the words of Prime Minister Blaize, "our rescuer after God."[119] Such is the difference between a people as they are and as totalitarians want them to be.

---

[118] Document 10533: Draft plan for Grenada-Cuba Cultural Agreement, 1981. Document 2293/100295: NJM Politburo minutes, 27 April 1983. Document 2033/00245: Grenada-DPRK agreement, 13 April 1983.
[119] *New York Times*, 21 February 1986, p.A-5.

3. The Party and the Economy

The question we must now pose, comrades, is whether a society such as ours with their [*sic*] primitiveness, with so little infrastructure, with so little development of productive forces, with such a small working class can really build socialism.

—*Maurice Bishop*
"Line of March" speech, 1982

As defined by Friedrich and Brzezinski, the totalitarian economy is characterized by its centralization in both planning and operation. There are limits to this definition; for example, while no one denies the totalitarian nature of Nazi Germany, it is often pointed out that the German economy was not fully centralized during the Third Reich. There is no doubt, however, that the economy operated in accordance with the wishes of Hitler, and was therefore centralized in effect, if not in fact. As Franz Borkenau noted, total centralization is unnecessary when the result is the same.[120]

The totalitarian ideology of Marxism-Leninism aims toward full control of the economy because, to the Marxist-Leninist, life *is* economics; it is therefore impossible to effect the transformation of society, even politically, if the populace still exercises bourgeois economic freedoms. In its 1973 *Manifesto*, the NJM recognized the unity of politics and economics with its observation that "it is necessary that we reject the present economic and political system which we live under." The Party professed a view of a completely new society, composed of new men with new values; no longer, the Party said, would men exploit each other because of their greed. "The creation of this new man demands the transformation of the minds and hearts of each and every one of us." Consistent with its subsequent commitment to Marxism-Leninism, the NJM equated economics with politics.[121]

Once in power, however, the Party hesitated from exercising complete state ownership and control. It recognized that a transition period was needed, much like Lenin's New Economic Policy, in which private and public ownership would exist side by side. Bernard Coard, finance minister and deputy prime minister, announced in the first month of the regime that "the Government has a mixed economy in mind" but also noted that private enterprise had to prove its superiority over public enterprise in order to be preserved. That coexistence was a temporary measure prior to full social-

---

[120] Franz Borkenau, *The Totalitarian Enemy* (London: Faber and Faber, 1940), pp.24, 197.
[121] NJM 1973 *Manifesto*, reprinted in *CMB*, April 1979, pp.26-52.

ism was made clear by Bishop in his 1982 "Line of March" speech to a general meeting of the Party. Bishop stated that free enterprise had been rejected as the state's ultimate economic goal because it would be "inconsistent with what we believe in and what we have been and are struggling for"; he stressed that "we could not likewise choose that path of the mixed economy" because "that will have tremendous dangers for the successful construction of Socialism." Total state ownership and control during the National Democratic stage of the Revolution, he said, was impossible "for the time being," because of the combined lack of an industrial infrastructure and the small size of Grenada's working class. Bishop also observed that the Party lacked the necessary managerial and planning skills necessary to maintain a completely socialist revolution:

For these primary reasons we cannot proceed straight away to the building of socialism but must first pass through a stage where we lay the basis, where we create the conditions . . . for the building of socialism and the creation of the socialist revolution, that is, for the full coming to power of the working class.[122]

Bishop therefore made it clear that the mixed economy was but a temporary stage designed "to consolidate and build the revolution." By September of 1982 the PRG had already, in accordance with the NJM plan, nationalized Grenada's banks, insurance companies, tourist agencies, utilities, and transportation facilities; still, Bishop lamented the fact that the state as yet controlled only one-quarter of the Grenadian economy. Party comrades were asked to be patient, and were told that full state control would depend on two factors; the building of an industrial infrastructure, and the development of a "central planning mechanism for the economy and the society as a whole." Prior to the establishment of an industrial base and fully centralized planning, the economy would necessarily retain elements of private enterprise. Making explicit reference to Lenin's New Economic Policy, Bishop warned against "nurturing the shoots of capitalism" during the transition stage.[123]

Fraternal Assistance

Toward its ultimate goal of a completely socialist economy, the New Jewel Movement sought and received economic assistance from the network of Soviet bloc and client states in three general areas: the creation of an industrial infrastructure; the development of central planning skills and mechanisms; and the deception of capitalist financial organizations.

Grenada's economy has always been overwhelmingly agricultural in nature; industry accounts for only five percent of the gross domestic product, and employs less than ten percent of the labor force. The Party sought to

---

[122] Document 12203: Bishop's "Line of March" speech to NJM, 13 September 1982.
[123] Ibid.

develop a larger industrial base for three reasons. First, the Party had to increase the number of workers in the state, in order to remain both consistent ideologically and to increase PRG control as the industrial sector developed. Second, in order to gain increased amounts of hard currency with which to buy arms or fund subversive activities in the region, the economy had to be expanded; Grenada's agricultural base was simply incapable of providing this expansion, as world demand for its principal export crop, nutmeg, remained stable. Third, an agricultural economy is subject to the non-dialectic vicissitudes of nature—namely the weather—and is therefore less subject to totalitarian will. This is especially true in tropical climes, where agricultural products are generally too fragile for long periods of storage and do not readily withstand hurricanes and other tropical storms.

At the same time, however, the Party recognized that agriculture would necessarily remain the major basis of the Grenadian economy for the foreseeable future. The solution, then—no doubt based on the Soviet experience—was the combined industrialization and collectivization of agriculture (the latter will be discussed shortly), with the concomitant development of certain elements of an industrial infrastructure.

For example, major farm machinery, irrigation and spraying equipment, and assistance in expanding the fruit, dairy and livestock "agro-industries," were to be provided by Cuba, East Germany, the USSR, Czechoslovakia, Bulgaria, and North Korea. Help in developing a fishing industry, including boats and training, was given by Cuba, North Korea, and East Germany. In addition, much Soviet bloc attention was directed toward Grenada's non-agricultural development. Cuba was building an island-wide road network. Czechoslovakia sent experts to help expand Grenada's ceramics industry. Bulgaria planned to build an ice plant. Hungary was funding the development of drug manufacturing. The USSR itself was to build a water supply system, a cement plant, a satellite telecommunications station, a hotel, and a power station in the 1984–1985 period alone; it was also to develop deep-water port facilities.[124]

Another crucial element of Soviet assistance necessary for the Party's socialist agenda was the development of centralized planning. The Documents indicate that as early as December 1979 Soviet economic and trade delegations were visiting the PRG to provide guidance. Officials from the PRG's Ministries of Planning, Trade, and Finance were sent to Cuba in 1981 and 1982 to receive instructions from Havana's *Junta Central de Planificacion* (Juceplan—the Cuban version of Gosplan, the Soviet State Planning

---

[124] Document 2033/00245: Grenada/DPRK "Protocol on the Economic and Technical Cooperation," 13 April 1983. Document 9207: Grenada/Czechoslovakia technical agreement, 5 October 1983. Document 11703: Coard draft letter to IMF, 1983. Document 2305/100364: NJM Central Committee Plenary minutes, 13-23 July 1983.

64

Committee) and from the Cuban National Bank. Areas of training included banking and finance under capitalism; finance under socialism; nationalization of the private banks; the relationship between banking and planning; and techniques of monetary control. Juceplan also provided training in controlling imports and exports, and in the use of computers in planning.

After Cuba had provided instruction in the more basic aspects of a centralized economy, a Soviet "technical delegation" visited Grenada in December 1982 to extend further guidance. This high-level delegation consisted of six officials from Gosplan—including its deputy chairman—and met at least eight times with NJM Politburo members. While the Soviets approved of the Party's plan to reduce the private sector, apparently they were also concerned with outward appearances; the Soviets warned against friction with capitalists that was "obvious" and recommended caution, lest the private sector appear too successful in contrast to state-owned operations. This was consistent with the NJM's strategy of not appearing to be a communist party. Apparently the Gosplan visit also laid the basis for economic training in the Soviet Union itself; by the following May, Grenadians from the Ministry of Trade were attending courses in the USSR.[125]

Despite the Party's agenda of socialist transformation, it was not above seeking economic assistance from the same capitalist organizations it vilified. The Party denounced President Reagan's Caribbean Basin Initiative (CBI), as neo-colonialism, for example, but all the same it tried to reap CBI benefits; in July of 1983 the Central Committee agreed to establish false private companies, in order to make Grenada's private sector appear larger and growing, so that the PRG would qualify for CBI assistance. The following month the Party leadership decided to extend this kind of economic deception to its efforts to receive further IMF loans. Bishop recommended, and the Party agreed, to solicit assistance from Cuba, Nicaragua, and Surinam in the keeping of alternate sets of records which would indicate a higher level of private sector profits and participation than actually existed or was planned. The Documents indicate the Party's certainty that the countries approached were practiced in deceiving international financial bodies—and its confidence that fraternal assistance in these techniques would be extended.[126]

---

[125] Document 12236: Agenda of PRG delegation to Juceplan, December 1981. Documents 12417 and 12418: Ministry of Planning letters to Havana, December 1981 and November 1982. Documents 5289 and 4943: Minutes of meetings with Gosplan officials, 21 and 23 December 1982. Document 12043: Ministry of Trade staff meeting, 20 May 1983.

[126] Document 2305/100364: NJM Central Committee Plenary minutes, 18-23 July 1983. Documents 2292/100283 and 6825: NJM Political and Economic Bureau minutes, 3 and 10 August 1983.

The Collectivization of Agriculture

It is in the area of agriculture that the Documents reveal most clearly the totalitarian bent of the New Jewel Movement. As noted earlier, the Grenadian economy is historically and predominantly agricultural in nature. Pending the eventual development of an industrial base, the Party recognized that economic reform consonant with its totalitarian ideology would focus on agriculture. Collectivization of agriculture was not only the key to ideological consistency and the means of bringing the most important sector of the economy under Party control; it is clear that the Party regarded collectivization as a practical instrument in eliminating political opposition.

Over 40% of Grenada's total land area is farmland. The Party was faced with a sizeable petty-bourgeois landowning opposition, in that there were over 8,000 separate farms of an average size of only four acres. Within a year of attaining state power, the Party began to put into motion a carefully orchestrated plan to bring both agriculture and potential opposition under its control.

In the first half of 1980, the Party's Land Reform Commission (a subcommittee of the NJM's Economic Bureau, and *not*, significantly, a state body) conducted extensive surveys of land holdings in the Grenadian countryside. The aim of these surveys was to identify those farms which would be initially subject to nationalization—although the Party insisted that the term to be used was "compulsory lease instead of acquisition or seizure." At that time the Party was planning to implement a law allowing the state to seize any land it deemed to be "idle," that is, not producing sufficiently. The Commission identified each land holding by its "alleged owner"; careful note was made of each landowner's "assessed capacity for cooperation" and political views. The Party identified over 11,000 acres, or about one-third of Grenada's farmland, for takeover. Of these, only 30 percent were held by owners identified by the Commission as a "Supporter" or "Neutral"; the rest were labeled "Anti-PRG," "Counter," or "Ex-Gairyite." The political implications were not lost on the Party:

. . . the present approach is to enact this Land Development and Utilization Law and under its powers to compulsorily lease 7,000 acres of land *which now belong to the most hostile elements of the landed bourgeoisie* . . . The additional 5,000 acres of land in plots over 100 acres belong to elements of the landed bourgeoisie who, although not supportive of the Revolution, are prepared to work with the Revolution and can be held in line *at this time.*[127]

As the Land Commission completed its surveys, the requisite law providing for state seizure of "idle lands" was enacted by the PRG in 1982.

---

[127] Document 6433: NJM agriculture report, 12 July 1983. Document 5528: NJM Land Reform Commission report, February or March 1980; emphasis added. See also Document 11620: Land Reform Commission report for June-October 1980. The terms of "compulsory leasing" were close to outright seizure: one per cent annually of the rent value, as determined by the PRG. See Document 7124: NJM Politburo minutes, 19 January 1983.

Between October 1982 and January 1983, the Party's Central Committee deliberated the land question. "The CC observed that if this question was not resolved urgently, the process of socialist orientation would be seriously retarded." The direction intended by the Party was clearly the eventual and complete collectivization of land under state ownership; the Party was reticent only in the pace of implementation. Like the question of religious freedom, the issue of socialist land reform was recognized as "explosive." Nevertheless, the Party resolved to place 6,000 acres under immediate state control; this land would be divided into eight "semi-autonomous regions," from which 36 state farms would be created. Ten farmers would be allowed to farm every 100 acres in cooperative fashion, with no employment of labor allowed. Quotas of specialized products would be established; those not meeting the plan would be removed from the land. These initial acts were identified by Bishop himself as "Priority No. 1" in the Party's strategy to:

a. Ensure the beginning of the collectivization of Agriculture and starting the process of the transformation of the countryside along socialist lines.

b. Serve to expand production in Agriculture as a means of creating the raw material and the finances for the further expansion of the industrial working class.

The timetable for the complete "transformation of the countryside" extended through December 1985.[128]

The Party was well aware of potential hostility to its plans. Rural Grenadian society was categorized by the Party into five classes, ranging from the "agro-proletariat" through the "semi-proletariat," the "small peasant" and "big peasant" to the "plantocracy." Although the support of the lower rural classes was expected from allowing them to work larger areas than those to which they were accustomed, the Party expected opposition from the upper two classes:

The upper peasants are under the political hegemony of the big planters and are generally hostile to the Revolution. . . . They cannot be encouraged to expand in any way and should be treated in the same way as the planters . . . the big planters [are] the remnants and the most backward strata of the old ruling class. They are openly hostile to the Revolution. . . .[129]

To the Party, of course, "hostility to the Revolution" meant that these farmers did not want to give up their land. The Party fully expected this class-based opposition; therefore,

Once the first [period] of the land reform is completed, *they will have to be smashed* in the second [period] and their lands turned over to the State. . . .[130]

---

[128] Document 2138/00184: NJM Central Committee minutes, 12-15 October 1982. See also Documents 6039 and 10778: NJM Central Committee draft resolutions on agriculture and land, with Bishop's notes, October 1982 and January 1983.

[129] Document 10778, ibid.

[130] Ibid.; emphasis added.

This pseudo-Leninist language gives Sovietologists a sense of deja vu, as it reminds one of the horrors of Soviet forced collectivization. Again, the Documents indicate the Party's long-term goals in this area; in July 1983, three months before the fall of the PRG, the Party noted approvingly that

. . . the acquisition of approximately 6,000 acres of land has been an important development. This land will further lay the basis for the modernization of agriculture and *the total destruction of the landowning class.*[131]

There can be no doubt that the Party was referring to forced collectivization. A document from the same month refers to the Party's plan to establish one huge state farm, of 10,000 to 15,000 acres, in the island's northeast section. This would require state seizure of the remaining 5,000 acres identified as "idle," plus the identification and acquisition of an additional 5,000 to 10,000 acres. This one state farm would cover a full third of Grenada's farmland, and the Party seemed determined to go to great lengths to acquire it.[132]

There is one document which not only seems to embody the Party's attitude to agriculture and the economy, but also indicates the price which a totalitarian party is willing to pay for the accomplishment of its objectives. Sometime in late 1982 or early 1983, Maurice Bishop led a Party study group which discussed the land question and the expected opposition to collectivization. With what must have been full knowledge of the horrible (yet ultimately victorious) Soviet experience with forced collectivization in the 1920s and 1930s, in his lesson plan Bishop made an explicit comparison between the Grenadian capital of St. George's and Moscow. Further,

There is a lot in common in the Soviet countryside and our own in Grenada.

(a) Large number of petty small scale producers.

(b) Absolute backwardness—petty bourgeois individualism, distrust for all that [is] new, low level of class consciousness and primitiveness of farming. . . .

Capitalism will not be undermined and defeated in the countryside until we establish fully the appropriate forms of collectivization as the alternate to small scale petty production.[133]

Under the heading "Class Forces and Their Role," Bishop asked the following questions:

What strategy and tactics do we have for crushing the Grenada Kulaks?

What is the attitude of the G'DA KULAKS to Revo at present?

---

[131] Document 8213: Workers' Committee report to NJM Central Committee Plenary, 13-19 July 1983.

[132] Document 6433: "Agriculture Production and Diversification," 12 July 1983.

[133] Document 4804: Maurice Bishop's Party Study Notebook.

For how long will it remain?

What is their role in the present stage?[134]

Unfortunately, the explicit answers were apparently not recorded; fortunately, the Party did not remain in power long enough to respond with deeds to the attitude of Grenada's "kulaks." We can only speculate, therefore, on the specific measures planned by the Party to implement its avowed policy of collectivization.

Though there is no "smoking gun" of conclusive evidence, it seems clear that the Party was making ready to impose forced collectivization at virtually any cost. The Party had already defined the socialist transformation of agriculture as a necessary step in creating the new society. Anticipated opponents of the Party's agrarian policy were identified as political adversaries. The Party used Leninist references in planning the "smashing" and "crushing" of these enemies. Finally, with explicit reference to the Soviet experience, these same enemies were labeled "kulaks."

Perhaps no other word in any language symbolizes the totalitarian's ruthless disdain for life. This Russian word for "fist" was in the Soviet experience applied not only to prosperous peasants, nor only to opponents of collectivization, but to those who simply refused to allow the expropriation of all their food. By declaring war on the kulaks and aiming for their "liquidation as a class," Stalin was able simultaneously to enforce collectivization and remove political opposition. This was particularly true in Ukraine, during the horrible "famine on command" of 1932–1933. The result was the death of at least seven million, and perhaps as many as fifteen million, Ukrainian peasants. The use of famine as an instrument of totalitarianism has been seen since in the cases of the Soviet client states of Ethiopia and Afghanistan; there is no reason to believe it will not be used again.[135] The use of this specific 1930s-era Soviet term—a euphemism for genocide—in a West Indian island in the 1980s is indeed ominous. It illustrates the fungibility of totalitarianism, its transcendent character which seems to need only evil as a common denominator.

---

[134] Ibid.

[135] The best work on the Ukrainian "famine on command" is Robert Conquest's recent *Harvest of Sorrow* (New York: Oxford University Press, 1986). For a survivor's account, see Miron Dolot, *Execution by Hunger* (New York: Norton, 1985). Despite the apparently incontrovertible evidence that Stalin's regime deliberately starved between 7 and 15 million Ukrainians to death, this horrible history is little known in the West; see Peter Paluch, "Spiking the Ukrainian Famine, Again," *National Review*, 11 April 1986.

4. Totalitarianism for Export

[Regarding] the supposedly secret documents that fell into the hands of the United States and were published by the Yankee administration . . . Nowhere in those documents that they have been crowing over is there anything that has to do with the idea of military bases in Grenada.

—*Fidel Castro, November 1983*[136]

In this final section the degree to which Grenada under the New Jewel Movement was expansionist in nature, or supportive of totalitarian expansion, will be examined. The compulsion of totalitarianism to expand until it engulfs the entire world was described by Franz Borkenau in 1940; explained as a combination of ideology and consistency by Hannah Arendt in the 1950s; and, in its Soviet manifestation, continues to be decried by Jean-François Revel in the 1980s. This section will show that the Grenadian contribution to Soviet expansionism had both military and political aspects, the latter more operationally active.

Much attention has already been drawn to the secret military agreements between the PRG and the Soviet Union, Cuba, North Korea, and Czechoslovakia; it is not, moreover, the intent of this monograph to duplicate the works edited by Romerstein and Ledeen, Seabury and McDougall, and Uri Ra'anan, et al. These publications well document the development of the PRG's armed forces into a formidable military threat in the region, as well as the stockpiling of weapons which—together with the completion of the famous (or perhaps infamous) international airport—were making Grenada a significant logistics and operations resource for Cuba and the Soviet Union. Romerstein and Ledeen, commenting on Grenada's armed forces, note that enough weapons were found on the island to support an army of 10,000. The Documents indicate that the PRG maintained a regular force of 3,000 men, already far larger than that of all Grenada's neighbors combined; St. Vincent and St. Lucia, for example, have no military whatsoever. This force could be rapidly expanded with militia to number 5,000. According to notes taken at a meeting between the PRA, a Cuban general, and Manuel Pineiro, head of the Cuban Central Committee's Americas Department, plans were made to increase even this force to almost 7,000, thereby making the PRA the largest military force in the world in terms of ratio to population.[137]

---

[136] Speech in Havana, 14 November 1983, reprinted in *Maurice Bishop Speaks*, pp.326-341.
[137] Document 2094/00051: "Wed. Meeting with Pineiro and General Lezcano," handwritten notes probably by Hudson Austin, undated.

However certain one may be about the eventual result of such a one-sided regional arms buildup, the available evidence that PRA troops were employed to further Soviet and Cuban interests remains circumstantial. Within weeks of the NJM *putsch*, the government of neighboring St. Vincent charged that 16 armed Grenadians had attempted to land on one of its smaller islands in order to support an insurrection there. The PRG vehemently denied the accusation; but later, in May 1980, it announced that 500 PRA soldiers would be sent to Namibia to fight alongside SWAPO. The following October, it was reported by a Trinidadian newspaper that several PRA troops had been killed while participating in Sandinista operations against the Miskito Indians. With the delivery of a Soviet Antonov-26 paratroop plane—ostensibly for VIP transport—the PRA would have had supremacy over its neighbors in the ability to project power. Despite these reports, so far there is no real evidence that the PRA saw any combat before U.S. and OECS forces invaded the island in October 1983.[138]

The case for the international airport being the PRG's primary contribution to Soviet and Cuban interests, however, is well documented. In the publications already cited, for example, there is the now well-known diary entry of PRG security chief Liam James: "The Revo has been able to crush Counter-Revolution internationally, airport will be used for Cuban and Soviet military," as well as Bishop's remark to Gromyko at their Moscow meeting that the airport was a potential threat to NATO supply routes. After an NJM Politburo member boasted publicly in February 1983 that the airport would be used by Cuba to supply their troops in Angola, *Newsweek* asked Bishop "to categorically state that the new airport . . . would never be used to tranship arms or other military supplies"; Bishop dodged the question and stated that it was a civilian project designed to increase economic prosperity.[139] There is little doubt that the Cuban-designed international airport, funded mainly by Soviet client states, figured into Soviet strategic planning: a PRG-Cuban agreement of September 1981 allowed Cuba to build a fuel farm at the airport which was to have a capacity of 1.5 million gallons. (In addition, Cuba was to build 20,000 square meters of warehouses and barracks to house 2,500 "students.")

That these facilities were definitely to be used for Soviet or Cuban military operations is shown by Bishop's request to Libyan strongman Muammar Quadhaffi to assist in funding the fuel farm, the purpose of which was not to provide refueling facilities for commercial air traffic, but

---

[138] See Timothy Ashby, "Grenada: Soviet Stepping Stone," U.S. Naval Institute *Proceedings*, December 1983.

[139] *Newsweek*, 13 June 1983. See also the *Washington Post*, 27 February 1983. Bishop said his government viewed the airport "in exactly the same way in which the United States saw the railways in the last century." He might have been telling the truth—the U.S. railways were planned with very different uses in peacetime and in war. See also Ra'anan, p.399, and Romerstein and Ledeen, document 23.

... storage tanks for 1.5 million gallons of diesel, kerosene, & aviation gas *to ensure that strategic supplies are available for emergency purposes.*[140]

The Libyan leader, himself a Soviet client, provided US$4 million for this cause. Finally, Liam James' diary records a meeting between Bishop, Coard, Austin, James, and General Ochoa of Cuba at which was discussed "[u]se of our airport in case of any emergency." Until an emergency presented itself, the airport would undoubtedly facilitate an increase in Grenada's sagging tourist trade, as well as provide the means for Castro to prop up his surrogate, Bishop, if the latter should run into domestic problems. In times of superpower crisis, on the other hand, the airport would allow the Soviet Union a wide range of strategic options. The potential for "horizontal escalation" in the region if there were military tensions in Europe, for example, are high: Cuban-piloted Soviet aircraft operating from Grenada could threaten the Panama Canal, oil fields and refineries in Venezuela and Trinidad, and Caribbean sea lanes through which pass the majority of U.S. oil imports. The Soviet Union was planning to install in Grenada an INTERSPUTNIK satellite dish telecommunications system for message traffic between Moscow, Havana, Managua, and St. George's—a system which would have to be in place prior to coordinated force deployment.[141]

Besides the military problem Grenada was to pose for U.S. strategic planners, Moscow also assigned the PRG an active political role. Party leaders exhibited political solidarity with the Sandinista junta of Nicaragua, which included sending NYO volunteers to Managua to assist the Sandinista literacy program and PRA officers to observe the war with the democratic resistance. The PRG voted with the Soviet Union in the UN— even opposing the vote condemning the destruction of KAL 007—and supported Soviet and Cuban interests both in the Socialist International and in the so-called Non-Aligned Movement (membership in which the NJM had managed to secure, despite the fact it was a communist party).[142]

The most important role assigned to the NJM, however, appears to have been as a center for the training of regional Marxist-Leninist parties from small island countries like Grenada, which hoped to repeat the NJM experience. Aside from the Cuban Communist Party and Guyana's People's

---

[140] Document 5169: Bishop request to Libyan Government, June 1982; emphasis added.

[141] Document 7125: PRG-Cuban agreement, 16 September 1981. Document 8343: Transcript of Liam James notes, undated. Document 12492: Report to Bishop from Ambassador Jacobs on Moscow meeting with the Soviet Minister of Post and Telecommunications, 30 May 1982. For U.S. strategic interests in the region, see *The Soviet-Cuban Connection in Central America and the Caribbean* (Washington, D.C.: USGPO, March 1985).

[142] Document 2095/00084: Major Roberts' letter to Ambassador Cornwall in Havana, undated. *CMB*, January 1982, p.31. Document 2293/100298: Report of PRG delegation to meeting of Non-Aligned Movement in Managua, 10-14 January 1983. Seabury and McDougall, documents VII-1 through VII-3. Romerstein and Ledeen, documents 33A, 34 through 35.

Progressive Party (PPP), there are no Caribbean Marxist-Leninist parties of electoral significance (though socialist parties are strong, particularly in Jamaica). According to one observer, the weak popular appeal of Marxist-Leninist ideology stems partly from its inability to transcend the deep ethnic, cultural, and social divisions in the region, as well as from the general distrust of university intellectuals which make up Caribbean Marxist-Leninist elites. As a result, most of the region's far left parties lacked political organization.[143] Clearly, the NJM coup, which had popular support mainly because of the excesses of Gairy, could be duplicated only with assistance from the PRG and Cuba.

Informational ties between the New Jewel Movement and the other leftist fringe groups in the area were established long before the NJM came to power in 1979. After the coup, the NJM became a sort of clearinghouse for information regarding the region's "progressive forces"; Bishop received detailed reports from Marxist-Leninist parties such as MONALI of Barbados, YULIMO of St. Vincent, and the Antigua Caribbean Liberation Movement on the political situation in the respective islands, including identification of enemies and sympathetic forces. Beginning in June of 1980 the Cuban Embassy in St. George's provided weekly analyses of the East Caribbean press which included identification of regional political trends and advice on official responses to significant articles; Cuba also allowed the PRG to collect information on regional movements from its embassy in Havana, and arranged meetings with members of Latin American "national liberation movements."[144] The PRG dutifully submitted this intelligence to Moscow, a service gratefully acknowledged by Gromyko, then Soviet foreign minister, to Bishop during their April 1983 meeting in Moscow:

Let me thank you for the very interesting and comprehensive information on your region . . . I will convey this information personally to Comrade Andropov who incidentally sends his warmest greetings, as well as to all my Comrades in the Soviet leadership.[145]

In November of 1981 the PRG hosted a Solidarity Conference attended by leftist parties from most of the countries of the Caribbean Basin. Also in attendance were representatives from the PLO, SWAPO, CPUSA, Covert Action USA, the USSR, Ethiopia, and the office of U.S. Congressman Ron Dellums. Apparently at this conference the groundwork was laid for future support and training of the region's Marxist-Leninist parties, as well as those groups known to be socialist in orientation. By mid-1982 Bishop was able to report to his Soviet mentors that such support was regular and proceeding well:

---

[143] W. Raymond Duncan, "Caribbean Leftism," *Problems of Communism*, May-June 1978, p.46.

[144] Documents 4057, 5175, 5294, 8869, 8872: Reports to the NJM from Caribbean Marxist-Leninist parties. Documents 2443/100642 and 6883: Cuban press analyses, 1980-1983. Document 5182: PRG Embassy in Havana workplan for 1983. See also Ra'anan, pp.391-94.

[145] Document 4708: Summary of Moscow meeting between Bishop and Soviet Foreign Minister Gromyko, 15 April 1983.

... we learn the experiences of our closest neighbours and help them in their organizational work as part of our international duty. Thus for example we have a standing agreement with the progressive and Revolutionary comrades in Surinam. Every six weeks we send to Surinam comrades in six areas of work. Party building, Security, Study in the Armed Forces, Propaganda, Developing the Mass Organizations, Studying and understanding the economy.[146]

By the time of Bishop's April 1983 meeting with Gromyko, he was able to report that NJM was holding regional seminars in organization and ideology twice yearly as part of its "international duty," and that the region's "progressive" parties were increasingly on a "Marxist-Leninist trend." Apparently the NJM was becoming known in the network of Soviet client states as the regional specialist; in late 1982 Libya requested NJM assistance in contacting seven leftist parties, ranging from the People's National Party of former Jamacian Prime Minister Michael Manley to the insignificant Progressive Labour Party of St. Lucia.[147]

One training conference, co-sponsored by the NJM and Trevor Munroe's Worker's Party of Jamaica (Marxist-Leninist), was held in Grenada in March of 1983. The five-day conference was attended by eleven leftist parties from nine Caribbean countries. (Interestingly, the Cubans seemed not to be in attendance, perhaps an indication that the NJM had graduated to independent operations.) The agenda included workshops on general propaganda techniques, agitation in trade unions, mobilization of women, creation of mass organizations, and "Leninist administration."[148]

At another such conference, the various participating parties gave presentations on topics useful to the political goals of the participants; specifically, the Leninist acquisition of power. The PPP of Guyana, for example, identified the importance of linking religion with the historical oppression of women when forming a women's mass organization; this had the dual objective of providing material for agitation while denigrating religion. The PPP cited the specific propaganda assistance available in this area from the Soviet Union. At the same conference, the Dominica Liberation Movement presented a paper on "The Struggle of the Peasantry," and the February 18th Movement of Trinidad and Tobago spoke on the importance of propaganda to Marxism-Leninism; Lenin was praised as "the master propagandist."

---

[146] Document 7082: "Presentation by the comrade leader to the Leadership of the Soviet Union," undated but probably mid-1982.

[147] Document 4939: Guest list for Solidarity Conference in Grenada, November 1981. Document 4708: Bishop-Gromyko meeting, 15 April 1983. Document 6825: NJM Politburo minutes, 27 October 1982. Romerstein and Ledeen, document 83.

[148] Document 10498: Agenda of regional leftist conference held in Grenada, 14-18 March 1983.

It was the presentation of the virtually unknown Worker's Revolutionary Movement of St. Lucia, however, which best reveals the New Jewel Movement's intentions in hosting these training sessions. In its paper on "Strategy and Tactics in [the] Electoral Struggle," the WRM recommended that parties aspiring to power should

[a]lways point out the deficiencies and built-in contradictions within the Westminister electoral system under which the election is taking place . . . The purpose is to tactically set the stage by pointing out that we must have no absolute confidence in this form of struggle as the best means of changing a government . . . to show people that *the electoral way is not the only way*, and that if and when it becomes impossible to reflect the genuine wishes of the people . . . *there are other ways which will have to be used to reflect the feelings and wishes of the people.*[149]

The New Jewel Movement's greatest operational contribution to the expansion of totalitarianism was its support and assistance of Caribbean leftist elites which aimed at skirting established legislative and electoral procedures in order to make a Leninist grab for power. The ideological and organizational development of these parties was accompanied by the growth of NJM's military arm, the PRA, to the point where substantial armed support of a coup was possible. The airport's potential use as a logistical and operational base for the Soviet bloc can be seen primarily as NJM's thanks to its Soviet and Cuban mentors in helping Grenada become the Cuba of the Lesser Antilles.

---

[149] Document 10508: Leftist conference papers, undated; emphasis added.

Conclusion: Totalitarianism and U.S. Policy

Reckless talk of repression and the totalitarian left is a complete misrepresentation of the truth and must be considered a fabrication of major proportions.

—PRG Official, March 1982[150]

Although this examination of the Grenada Documents appears to offer a mixed assessment of totalitarianism in Grenada during the regime of the New Jewel Movement, the lessons of the Grenada experience for U.S. hemispheric policy are unambiguous.

Using the seven characteristics of the totalitarian state presented in the introduction—standards developed by Hannah Arendt, Carl Friedrich, and Zbigniew Brzezinski—it could be argued that the Grenada of the PRG does not qualify as a totalitarian state. The Documents indicate that in areas of both structure and policy, Grenada in the period from March 1979 to October 1983 fell short of most models of a truly totalitarian state. Most significantly, especially from Hannah Arendt's emphasis on totalitarianism as the greatest manifestation of evil in history, the leaders of the NJM did not initiate a systematic, all-encompassing campaign of terror, mounting in both scope and randomness of selection of victims, against the population at large. Though relatively large numbers of people were incarcerated because of their real or suspected political opposition to the Party, few if any were executed. Though there is evidence that torture of political and other prisoners did occur with some regularity, apparently this was not a policy decision on the part of the Party leadership.

Special note must be made of the peculiarly benign attitude—at least as compared with fully totalitarian systems—of the NJM with respect to the group which the Party identified as its primary adversary—organized and independent religion. Despite the operations conducted against Grenada's churches, detailed in these pages, little or no violence was exercised against clergy, congregations, or lay church officials.

PRG police structure is yet another anomaly from the totalitarian norm. Special Branch, the secret police, was a small organization, concerned mostly with surveillance operations. The role of the regular Police Service was almost exclusively directed against criminal activity. Contrary to the totalitarian model provided by the Nazi and Soviet experiences, in Grenada

---

[150] Deputy Finance Minister Ramdhanny, addressing U.S. Congressmen, quoted in CMB, April 1982, pp.32-33.

the PRA, the military arm of the NJM, retained the honor and position of "the defenders of the Revolution," or in Soviet parlance "the sword and shield of the Party." It was perhaps this failure of the Party leadership to establish a separate, strong secret police and intelligence agency which led to the transformation of the Party's internal power struggle into the open and violent palace revolution of October 1983—a development which, as Arendt observes, does not happen in fully totalitarian regimes.

In direction and intent, however, a persuasive case may be made that Grenada was being turned into a totalitarian state. Given that Marxism-Leninism is an absolute, messianic ideology, and with the NJM's early and unequivocal commitment to this ideology, Grenada's movement toward totalitarianism was predetermined prior to the moment when the NJM took power. In a self-conscious imitation of the Bolshevik example, the NJM was an elitist "vanguard" Party based on Leninist discipline and tactics which engaged in constant deception designed to mask its true nature, and which attained power not as a result of a popular movement, as claimed, but by force. Once in power, the Party proceeded to implement its program to create the "new man" in the "new Grenada." The Party aimed at nothing less than the radical transformation of society along the lines defined by its ideology.

The actions taken by the Party during its reign confirm its totalitarian intent. The Party was in total control of all state functions, and sought to expand state activity over all areas of Grenadian life in order to control Grenadian society fully. The Party kept itself separate from the PRG, using the state as a facade of legitimacy and an instrument of power. Likewise the military, the police services, the school system, the unions, the media, mass organizations, and the economy, were all regarded by the Party as instruments to be controlled or manipulated to its will. The Party's monopoly over the means of mass communications began early, along with a monopoly of the means of armed combat. In order to transform society, the Party steadily increased its control of the communication of ideas; starting with its use of the media, the Party aimed to politicize and reeducate the "backward" masses by its domination over the education of children, the establishment of the adult literacy program, the creation of mass organizations for youth, women, workers, and farmers, and even the transformation of Grenadian culture into an ideological instrument.

Opposition to the Party, both real and suspected, was simply defined as false consciousness and in no way reflective of the true attitude of the Grenadian people in whose name the Party purported to rule. There is evidence that near the end of its reign the Party was planning to supplant the existing churches of Grenada with one based on liberation theology and under Party control; likewise, in its twilight months the Party was developing a forced reeducation program for dissidents based on the Vietnamese and

Cuban experiences. There is also evidence that the Party planned to expand the size and capability of its police organizations so that they could more effectively conduct operations against real and potential opponents. Of course, these are actions completely consistent with a totalitarian ideology which states that man, to quote Rousseau, "shall be forced to be free."

The ever-increasing Party control of the Grenadian economy best crystallizes the totalitarian intent of the NJM leadership. Going far beyond nationalization and the expansion of the means of industrial production, the Party's goals were to control completely, and eventually transform, Grenada's predominantly agricultural economy. The Documents indicate that the Party was planning a program of forced collectivization, not only in order to bring agricultural production and profits under Party control, but finally to eliminate the political opposition expected from landowners—labeled the "Grenada kulaks" by the Party leadership.

Finally, the Party was actively supporting the spread of totalitarianism by its political support and training of Marxist-Leninist parties in the Caribbean as well as its development of the military potential to support by force Leninist takeovers in the region. As a self-professed loyal member of the Soviet network of surrogate and client states, the PRG assisted Soviet and Cuban interests in the export of revolution by providing a strategically significant operational and logistical base.

Ultimately, the question of a totalitarian Grenada is a judgment call, subject not only to one's personal criteria of what makes a totalitarian state, but also to whether one believes that intention constitutes essence. On balance it is clear that, in intention and direction, Grenada under the New Jewel Movement was indeed a totalitarian state. By itself, this conclusion is of marginal interest; but inherent in it are important implications.

The question of the development of totalitarianism in the small Carribbean island of Grenada between 1979 and 1983 is more than an intellectual exercise or historical curiosity. It is only pointing out the obvious to note that, since the late 1950s, the global political stage has witnessed a remarkable growth in the number of countries which are somehow allied to or have special relationships with the Soviet Union. Simultaneously, a variety of different cultures with diverse historical patterns have become characterized by essentially the same form of government—never from the expression of free choice in a democratic election, but instead from the violent seizure of control. For a time, Grenada was added to the ranks of countries such as Ethiopia, Nicaragua, Poland, Angola, and North Korea. Yet only from Grenada have Western scholars been provided with so open a window on the inner workings of such a government.

Unfortunately for the sake of justice, the historical record has been somewhat kind to totalitarian governments. Because of the control on information exercised by such closed societies, the degree of repression in and the threat of expansion posed by totalitarian states goes relatively unpublicized. The world is far more aware of human rights abuses in South Africa, for example, than of the much sadder situation in Cuba (although the recent campaign at the United Nations by U.S. Ambassador Vernon Walters to bring attention to the Cuban Gulag is noteworthy). As abhorrent as its racial policies are, its lack of a consistent, all-encompassing ideology or an expansionist tendency sets South Africa outside the class of totalitarian governments, and render unlikely its evolution in this direction.

Totalitarian states represent the greatest threat to justice and peace in the world. Totalitarian ideology demands that all opposition, foreign and domestic, be crushed and thrown onto the ash-heap of history; this justifies both its internal repression and outward expansion.

Because ideology is the very *raison d'etre* of totalitarian parties, the states which they rule cannot merely reform themselves along democratic lines. Sadly, history suggests strongly that totalitarian states, which always emerge through violence, must be defeated by violence.[151] Paradoxically, it is the peace-loving states which must resort to force in order to defend themselves from the totalitarian menace.

The United States, due to its position as the most powerful democracy the world has known, has a special responsibility to confront and defeat the implacable threat of totalitarianism. Unfortunately, the historical record has also been unkind to the United States in this regard. Although the totalitarian Axis was defeated in World War II, all Eastern and much of Central Europe was lost to a totalitarian ally, the USSR. Although the South Koreans were saved from their totalitarian brethren, it was at least partly out of fear of totalitarian China that the United States did not liberate the North. To this day Americans are profoundly embarrassed by the Bay of Pigs affair, not because it was only a half-hearted attempt to root out a totalitarianism growing in our own hemisphere, but because it was attempted at all. Although popular mythology has it that the United States "won" the conflict known as the Cuban Missile Crisis, in reality the United States agreed, in the final analysis, to allow the consolidation and maturation of a totalitarian Soviet client state which continues to threaten hemispheric stability. South Vietnam was lost because the United States did not recognize the totalitarian nature of the enemy, and in any case had not the will to confront and defeat it. Although prior to Operation Urgent Fury President Reagan had warned of the growing totalitarian threat in Grenada, even in this case actual intervention was justified largely as a rescue of American medical students.

Today, in Central America, a totalitarian movement under the sponsorship of the Soviet Union and Cuba is simultaneously attempting to consolidate its power in Nicaragua and to foment unrest in the region so that all Central

---

[151] See Jeane Kirkpatrick's seminal title essay in her *Dictatorships and Double Standards*.

America can be united under its "enlightened" ideology of *Sandinismo*, an alias for Marxism-Leninism. And yet, far from recognizing the totalitarian threat, the American people and their Congress remain bitterly divided, both over the nature of the beast and the appropriate response to its actions. To the credit of the current administration, even the most outspoken opponents of its Central American policy now admit that the Sandinistas are Marxist-Leninists; however, there remains an insufficient appreciation of the implications of this assessment. It is simply not enough to know that the Sandinistas are Marxist-Leninists in thin disguise; the American people must be educated in the essence of totalitarian theory and the challenges it presents to U.S. foreign policy.

This monograph attempts, it is hoped successfully, to make a small step toward this objective. If it can be established, for instance, that the Sandinistas are totalitarians, then it can be argued not only that the Nicaraguan people will suffer to a greater degree than under the merely authoritarian Somoza, but also that Nicaragua's neighbors, and ultimately the United States, are in danger. If the Sandinistas are totalitarians we can show that, despite the recent promises given by Daniel Ortega in signing the so-called Arias peace plan, Nicaragua cannot reasonably be expected to become a democratic society, enjoying the inalienable rights of freedom of speech and the press, freedom of worship, freedom of conscience and assembly which characterize such regimes. At best, we could expect the Sandinistas to beautify the totalitarian framework with a veneer of liberty, having the grain of nominal but highly publicized "freedoms," but a structure which would make possible the continued and unhindered pursuit of the ends inherent in a totalitarian system.

As yet, there is no Sandinista archive with which to evaluate the current Nicaraguan government. This is a situation that the democratic resistance, or Contra forces, fervently wishes to change. Nevertheless, there is more than enough evidence to conclude that the Nicaragua of the Sandinista National Liberation Front (FSLN) is a truly totalitarian state. This evidence has been brought to light through defectors from the FSLN, secret documents and speeches by the Sandinista leadership which have been smuggled out of Nicaragua, and by the objective, conscientious reporting of some Western correspondents. No attempt is made here of presenting all this evidence; what follows is merely representative of the material available.

Sandinista Ideology

According to Humberto Belli, a former Sandinista militant who converted to Christianity, since its beginnings in 1960 the FSLN has been a Marxist-Leninist party devoted to the development of a "new man" freed of corrupt bourgeois values; those who disagree with the FSLN are held to suffer from the false consciousness of these same bourgeois values. As Comandante and Defense Minister Humberto Ortega told his officers in June of 1981:

. . . we are guided by the Marxist-Leninist scientific doctrine of the Revolution . . . Marxism-Leninism is the scientific doctrine that guides our revolution, the instrument of analysis of our Vanguard for understanding [the revolution's] historic process and for carrying out the revolution . . . [152]

The political situation in Sandinista Nicaragua is best summarized by the Inter-American Commission on Human Rights, an agency of the Organization of American States: "There is no atmosphere of respect and tolerance for persons who profess other than official beliefs and ideologies."[153]

Over the years the FSLN has sought to conceal its ideological nature, instead emphasizing the factional divisions of the FSLN which existed in the mid-1970s. But in her acclaimed work *Nicaragua: Revolution in the Family*, Shirley Christian states that "the differences among [the comandantes] that had produced the split into three FSLN factions in 1975 had to do with strategies for reaching power, not philosophy of government." Unfortunately, the Western media have also focused on these divisions of the past, which involved the means and not the ends of armed struggle, and have even portrayed certain members of the ruling National Directorate (DN) as political moderates.[154] What the comandantes fear most is that the totalitarian nature of their revolution will be recognized, for then the danger to hemispheric stability will be revealed and United States intervention will then be justified. A 1977 FSLN statement warned:

Once the People's Sandinista Revolution has achieved its purpose of ousting the dictatorship and installing the People's Revolutionary Government, we will be able to develop openly along progressive Marxist-Leninist lines.

Similarly, DN member Bayardo Arce stated in a 1984 secret speech:

We have not declared ourselves Marxist-Leninists publicly. . . . Our strategic allies tell us not to declare ourselves Marxist-Leninists. . . . [155]

The FSLN as Vanguard Party

The Sandinistas regard their party, the FSLN, as the vanguard of the Revolution. The FSLN has long defined itself as the only true voice of the working people of Nicaragua, accountable to no one but itself. All opposi-

---

[152] Quoted in Shirley Christian, *Nicaragua: Revolution in the Family* (New York: Vintage Books, 1986), p.222. See also Humberto Belli, *Breaking Faith: The Sandinista Revolution and Its Impact on Freedom and Christian Faith in Nicaragua* (Winchester, IL: Crossway Books, 1986), chapter 1.

[153] Nina H. Shea, "Human Rights in Nicaragua," *New Republic*, 1 September 1986, pp.21-23.

[154] See, for example, Stephen Kinzer, "Top Sandinista: Ortega's Grasp Becomes Firmer," *New York Times*, 2 March 1987, p.A1. Christian, p.150.

[155] "General Political and Military Platform of the FSLN," 1977, quoted in John Norton Moore, *The Secret War in Central America* (Fredrick, MD: University Publications, 1987), p.14. Arce quoted in ibid., p.47.

tion to the FSLN comes from the reactionary bourgeoisie aided by the imperialistic United States—the "enemy of humanity," as defined by the Sandinista anthem. Consequently, the Sandinistas regard all state, cultural, media, and educational organizations not as expressions of a pluralistic democracy, but merely as instruments of the Party in its efforts to consolidate its hold on Nicaraguan society.

One of the most important documents to emerge from Sandinista Nicaragua is the "72-Hour Document," an internal FSLN report on a three-day meeting held in July, 1979, two months after the Sandinistas took power. In this revealing document the FSLN constantly refers to itself as "the vanguard" which "leads the class struggle and guides the whole nation":

. . . our people, led by the FSLN, are victoriously marching toward the sun of our historical and total liberation . . . This Party, which has a definite class position, a unique political principle, a scientific ideology, and a correct strategy and tactic, places itself at the forefront of all society. . . .

Within this important document is a statement which makes clear the totalitarian ends of the Sandinistas (or, indeed, any Marxist-Leninist party).

We are an organization which, at the head of its people, has seized power . . . We are an organization whose *greatest aspiration* is to maintain revolutionary power . . . Consequently, our goal is to work to educate our people to recognize their vanguard and the tasks it has proposed. . . .[156]

Toward the primary end of maintaining power, the totalitarian party aims at transforming society to accept its vanguard role. Through the watchdog Sandinista Defense Committees (CDS) (administered by the Sandinista secret police, or DGSE), and the militant *turbas divinas* ("divine mobs"), sources of opposition in the media, the Church, and in labor unions are routinely placed under surveillance, harassed, beaten, and even killed, all in the name of the vanguard. The Sandinista campaigns against the opposition newspaper *La Prensa* (just one of nine publications closed down by the Party), the traditional Catholic Church led by Cardinal Obando y Bravo, the non-Sandinista labor unions, and opposition political parties, have been documented in depth elsewhere.[157]

It should be pointed out, however, that the Sandinistas themselves acknowledge that a pluralistic democracy with popular representation is the last thing they desire. In the "72-Hour Document," the Sandinistas make clear that any political participation by groups other than the FSLN is merely a tactic of deception:

---

[156] "Analysis of the Situation and Tasks of the Sandinista People's Revolution," published as "The 72-Hour Document," U.S. Department of State, February 1986; emphasis added.

[157] See Shea, Belli, Christian, *passim*, as well as Robert S. Leiken (who once supported the Sandinistas), "Nicaragua's Untold Stories," *New Republic*, 8 October 1984, pp.16-23. See also Jaime Chamorro, "How 'La Prensa' Was Silenced," *Commentary*, January 1987, pp.39-44. Of particular interest are the revelations of a former Sandinista counterintelligence officer, Miguel Bolaños Hunter, in Ra'anan, *Hydra of Carnage*, pp.309-320, who confirms that the Catholic Church is considered "enemy number one" by the Sandinistas.

... the alliance that took the form of the Government of National Reconciliation ... was dictated by the need to neutralize Yankee interventionist policies in light of the imminent Sandinista victory. Actually, the selection and organization of the government was a relatively easy task, as it did not have to be negotiated with the opposition parties of the bourgeoisie, but merely involved appointing patriotic figures who were somewhat representative.

The document goes on to state that those opposition groups which cannot be directly co-opted will be infiltrated for the purpose of "assimilation."[158]

In order to give a semblance of political accountability without real substance, the Sandinistas have established "Face the People" meetings, in accordance with their 1969 Party manifesto, between local communities and Party officials. These are similar to the PRG's Zonal Councils. Complaints directed at Sandinista policy are, to say the least, discouraged; ration cards are collected before these meetings, and anyone brave enough to risk hunger with an inappropriate question is imprisoned.[159]

The elections of November 1984, lauded by many in the West, were similarly a measure to consolidate FSLN power behind a mask of democracy. In his secret speech of May 1984, Comandante Bayardo Arce assured his "comrades" that, because the Revolution required the power of the dictatorship of the proletariat,

... the ability of the class to impose its will using the instruments at hand, without going into formal or bourgeois details [means that] the elections are bothersome to us. ...

Arce went on to say that the Sandinistas were hoping by the elections to defuse the pressure from the United States (clearly, the invasion of Grenada had made an impact); once the usefulness of "this facade of pluralism" had ended, it would be eliminated. Consistent with these and many other similar statements made by the Sandinista leadership, the elections were a sham and "do not deserve to be dignified by that name," according to the liberal French newspaper *Le Monde*.[160]

In order to quell the growing discontent within Nicaraguan society, the Sandinistas have maintained from their earliest days in power a vast machinery of repression, consisting of the Cuban-trained secret police (DGSE), the ubiquitous Sandinista Army (an arm of the Party rather than of the state), the *turbas* and CDS civilian groups, and the Prison Administration, controlled by Minister of the Interior Tomás Borge. Today in Nicaragua there are at least 3,500 political prisoners, as well as 2,500 former National Guardsmen, in Sandinista jails; the prisons of the hated dictator Somoza held about 600 political prisoners. The Sandinista regime holds more prisoners of conscience than any other in the Western hemisphere, with the exception of Cuba. According to many Nicaraguan refugees, including

---

[158] "The 72-Hour Document," pp.5, 12.
[159] Leiken, p.19. For the rights guaranteed by the 1969 FSLN manifesto, see Belli, pp.16-17.
[160] Christian, pp.346-47; Belli, pp.55-70.

former Sandinista counterintelligence officer Miguel Bolaños, the physical and psychological torture of political prisoners is routine policy. Arrest may be the result of anonymous denunciation, religious worship in a non-progressive church, or percieved opposition to Sandinista policy. Hundreds of prisoners are held without charges, especially those persons who were in opposition political groups or non-Sandinista labor unions. There continues to be no right to privacy, to travel, or to assemble without authorization. Nicaragua, in short, is ruled by terror; as the Sandinistas boasted in 1979,

The reactionary bourgeoisie are defenseless, knowing by class intuition that its fate can depend on a telephone call.[161]

Despite the recent promises made by the Sandinistas that they will respect the peace plan signed in August 1987 and establish democratic pluralism with full political rights for all Nicaraguans, it is unlikely that this totalitarian movement will be the first in history to reform a totalitarian state by peaceful means. As a hint of things to come, when the re-opening of *La Prensa* was announced with much fanfare in September 1987, the FSLN stated that the paper could now operate "without any other restrictions than those imposed by the responsible exercise of journalism." (One recalls Maurice Bishop's slogan, "Long Live Responsible Journalism!") FSLN veteran Victor Tirado warned Party members to "prepare for political-ideological struggle. Clear revolutionary ideas must be made to triumph over backward ones." If this is not enough to indicate to *La Prensa*'s editors what the limits of "responsible journalism" are, Comandante Arce made it abundantly clear with his recent statement that the *turbas* have the right "to demonstrate our overwhelming majority." Only the pro-Sandinista *turbas*, it seems, have this right to demonstrate. A public demonstration of free speech within days of the signing of the Arias peace plan was broken up by police with dogs, stun guns, and riot sticks; 15 people were arrested. As of this writing (late October 1987), the prospects for a free and independent Nicaraguan media look dim; requests for licenses to begin new radio and television programming have been ignored by the Sandinista government, and the re-opened Catholic radio station is still forbidden to broadcast news. That *La Prensa* will push for freedom of the press there is no doubt; as editor Jaime Chamorro said in September 1987,

---

[161] "The 72-Hour Document," p.9; Shea, p.21; *New York Times*, 25 February 1987, p.A3; "Inside Communist Nicaragua: The Miguel Bolaños Transcripts," Heritage Foundation *Backgrounder* #294, 30 September 1983. See also "Sandinista Prisons: A Tool of Intimidation," U.S. Department of State, August 1986.

The Sandinistas say they expect us to practice responsible journalism, but it is not irresponsible to write that their dictatorship is a dictatorship.[162]

Unfortunately, there can also be no doubt that the Sandinistas will continue to show their totalitarian colors; the alternative is political suicide.

Sandinista Expansion

As a totalitarian state in the making, Nicaragua under the Sandinistas is by nature a threat to its neighbors. The Marxist-Leninists who now rule Nicaragua cannot but regard the neighboring democracies of Central America as threats to Sandinista legitimacy, and hence as targets for totalitarian consolidation. Apologists for the Sandinistas explain away statements such as Tomás Borge's ("This revolution goes beyond our borders") as mere rhetoric by a hard-line ideologue.[163] Unfortunately, the evidence is unequivocal on the danger posed by Sandinista totalitarianism to Central American democracy.

As a general rule, a pre-revolutionary totalitarian movement is quite open about its goals; long before coming to power Hitler, Lenin, Khomeini and, as we have seen, even the Grenadian NJM were not shy in laying out their plans for the new society. The Sandinistas are no exception, even on the subject of expansion. In its 1969 manifesto, for example, the FSLN vowed to struggle for a "true union of the Central American peoples within one country." Now in power, the Sandinistas are vigorously pursuing this goal. According to Edén Pastora, former Sandinista official and the famous "Commander Zero" of the Revolution, Sandinista Defense Minister Humberto Ortega plans to arm a unified Central America. Toward this end, and with massive assistance from Cuba (which itself has hemispheric interests), the Sandinistas are supporting communist insurgent movements and terrorist groups throughout Central and South America in order to destabilize the new and fragile democracies of the Western Hemisphere. These groups, which include not only the Marxist FMLN of El Salvador, the EGP of Guatemala, and the Popular Vanguard Party of Costa Rica, but also the M-19 of Colombia and the Montaneros of Argentina, operate from Managua and receive training and support from a network of Cuban, Libyan, Vietnamese, and even PLO personnel.

Along with its support for the region's "national liberation movements," Sandinista Nicaragua appears ready for a conventional military showdown with its neighbors; Miguel Bolaños states that Sandinista plans include the

---

[162] "Managua Lifts Ban on Opposition Paper," *New York Times*, 21 September 1987, p.A3; "Managua Braces for Return of Dissent," *New York Times*, 20 September 1987, p.A3; "Notebook," *New Republic*, 7 September 1987, p. 9; "Sandinistas Ban Station's Plan for Radio News," *New York Times*, 20 October 1987, p.A13; "Press Curbs Remain, Nicaraguan Editor Says," *New York Times*, p.A10.

[163] Quoted in *Newsweek*, 29 April 1985, p.46.

defeat of Honduras through a pretext, perhaps a Contra attack. Nicaragua might then occupy Honduras at the request of a pro-Sandinista "provisional government." Long before the Contras existed as a threat, the Sandinistas, with Soviet and Cuban help, had built up the Nicaraguan military to a level six times that of Somoza's rule; today, the Sandinista military outnumbers that of any of the Central American democracies, with an active duty force of 75,000, and a reserve and militia force of 54,000; there are plans to increase the total number of men under arms to 200,000. El Salvador, by comparison, has 22,000 active duty troops. It is no wonder that a recent poll by CID, a Costa Rican affiliate of the well-respected Gallup International, found that an overwhelming majority of Costa Ricans, Hondurans, Guate-malans, and Salvadorans approve of U.S. military aid to the Nicaraguan democratic resistance.[164]

That Sandinista Nicaragua is a totalitarian entity consolidating its power under the sponsorship of the network of Soviet client states is cause for even greater alarm for the United States. According to Bolaños, the Cubans actually run the DGSE, the Sandinista secret police (which is a direct copy of their own DGI); they also direct the reeducation of Nicaraguan society through the FSLN propaganda machine. Within the secret police and the Sandinista army, we again see the totalitarian "division of labor": in the DGSE Cubans assist in interrogations and torture; East Germans are involved in bugging and wiretappings (and also lend a hand in psycho-logical torture); and Bulgarians are charged with intelligence analysis. The Sandinista military also receives in-country training from PLO and Vietnam-ese *internacionalistas*, medical support from North Koreans, and special-ized training from Libyans in "special operations" such as kidnappings and assassinations. Abroad, Cuba provides instruction in intelligence, artillery, and tank warfare, and Bulgaria is known to be training Sandinista pilots to fly MiGs. There are currently 7,000 Cuban military and civilian advisors in Nicaragua, and over 12,000 Soviet advisors; their purpose is to help the FSLN strengthen its totalitarian grasp on Nicaraguan society and accom-plish its eventual goal of a Sandinista Central American "people's republic."[165]

In return for this assistance, the Sandinistas and their Cuban mentors willingly play an important role in Soviet regional strategy vis-a-vis the United States. Of course, the mass exodus of humanity which always

[164] Moore, chapter II, "Background of the Central American Conflict." "Bolaños Transcripts," Heritage Foundation. See the Fletcher School's Oral History Project interviews with Miguel Bolaños and Edén Pastora in *Hydra of Carnage*, pp.309-332. See also "The Challenge to Democracy in Central America," U.S. Departments of State and Defense, 2nd printing October 1986; and Morton Kondracke, "Who Wants Peace," *New Republic*, 28 September 1987.

[165] Moore, pp.6-7. Bolaños and Pastora in *Hydra of Carnage*, pp.311-12, 313-16, 326-29.

accompanies the consolidation of totalitarianism would mean the further destabilization of Mexico; and, according to Bolaños, the Cubans have planned that "[i]n long term strategy, Mexico is slated to be the last country to fall."[166]

Already there are over 200,000 Nicaraguans in the United States seeking refuge from totalitarianism; with the toppling of Central America and then Mexico, the United States would be faced with tens of millions of refugees, a situation of "horizontal escalation" which may rob the United States of the political will to respond to Soviet aggression elsewhere, even in Western Europe. The Soviet Union considers its long-term investment in Sandinista Nicaragua to be a good one; for example, the Punta Hueta airfield north of Managua, just one of four airfields built with Soviet aid, cost $100 million— the equivalent of one year's aid to the Nicaraguan resistance. Although Nicaragua has no need of this airfield, which has the longest runway in Central America, Punta Hueta would be ideal as a base for Soviet long-range bombers, ASW, and surveillance aircraft which cannot at present cover the Pacific coast of North America from Soviet Far Eastern bases. Jet aircraft operating from Nicaragua could also threaten the nearby Panama Canal and Caribbean shipping lanes, upon which the United States relies for the resupply of NATO in case of war. It is clear that, despite U.S. warnings about the introduction of high-performance jet aircraft into the region, the Sandinistas plan to acquire MiGs; as Daniel Ortega stated in August 1987, "We have the airfield, we have the men."[167]

U.S. Policy

Despite the clear recognition by the Reagan Administration of the Sandinista threat to hemispheric stability, the Administration has thus far done a poor job in educating the American public in the dire significance of the Central American situation. That so far the best spokesman for the Administration's position has been Oliver North is hardly indicative of a determined and consistent effort to publicize the Sandinistas as the totalitarians they are.

The concept of totalitarianism is not difficult to comprehend, and the characteristics by which it may be recognized are easily understood. The Grenada Documents have provided scholars with a window on totalitarianism in the Western Hemisphere, and these Documents should be used to educate the public and the Congress of the United States in the basics of

---

[166] Bolaños, in *Hydra of Carnage*, pp.717-720.

[167] "U.S. Fears Soviet Use of New Nicaraguan Airfield," *New York Times*, 26 July 1987, p.14; "Nicaragua Says It Will Proceed With Plans to get MiGs," *Washington Post*, 3 August 1987, p.A17. Bolaños states that the Punta Hueta base also has a Cuban school for sabotage where Guatemalan and Salvadoran guerrillas are trained. Penn Kemble and Arturo Cruz, "How the Nicaraguan Resistance Can Win," *Commentary*, December 1986, p.22.

totalitarian theory. Once this is accomplished, the totalitarian intentions of the Sandinistas will become evident through their own statements and actions, and at last consensus on U.S. policy in Central America may be achieved.

Much work remains to be done with the Grenada Documents. Although the Documents chronicle the actions, policies, and plans of an elite which ruled a small island for a brief period, further research can be of great use not only to scholars but to Western decisionmakers. Sufficient attention to this valuable resource will provide greater insights into the nature and intent of governments which are not only of current interest, such as Nicaragua and Cuba, but which are potential targets of totalitarianism—such as El Salvador, South Africa, or any of the Caribbean island-states which contain an antitype of the New Jewel Movement.

PERGAMON-BRASSEY'S
International Defense Publishers

List of Publications
published for the
Institute for Foreign Policy Analysis, Inc.

Orders for the following titles should be addressed to: Pergamon-Brassey's, Maxwell House, Fairview Park, Elmsford, New York, 10523; or to Pergamon-Brassey's, Headington Hill Hall, Oxford, OX3 0BW, England.

Foreign Policy Reports

ETHICS, DETERRENCE, AND NATIONAL SECURITY. By James E. Dougherty, Midge Decter, Pierre Hassner, Laurence Martin, Michael Novak, and Vladimir Bukovsky. 1985. xvi, 91pp. $9.95.

AMERICAN SEA POWER AND GLOBAL STRATEGY. By Robert J. Hanks. 1985. viii, 92pp. $9.95.

DECISION-MAKING IN COMMUNIST COUNTRIES: AN INSIDE VIEW. By Jan Sejna and Joseph D. Douglass, Jr. 1986. xii, 75pp. $9.95.

NATIONAL SECURITY: ETHICS, STRATEGY, AND POLITICS. A LAYMAN'S PRIMER. By Robert L. Pfaltzgraff, Jr. 1986. v, 37pp. $9.95.

DETERRING CHEMICAL WARFARE: U.S. POLICY OPTIONS FOR THE 1990S. By Hugh Stringer. 1986. xii, 71pp. $9.95.

THE CRISIS OF COMMUNISM: ITS MEANING, ORIGINS, AND PHASES. By Rett R. Ludwikowski. 1986. xii, 79pp. $9.95.

TRANSATLANTIC DISCORD AND NATO'S CRISIS OF COHESION. By Peter H. Langer. 1986. viii, 89pp. $9.95.

THE REORGANIZATION OF THE JOINT CHIEFS OF STAFF: A CRITICAL ANALYSIS. Contributions by Allan R. Millett, Mackubin Thomas Owens, Bernard E. Trainor, Edward C. Meyer, and Robert Murray. 1986. xi, 67pp. $9.95.

THE SOVIET PERSPECTIVE ON THE STRATEGIC DEFENSE INITIATIVE. By Dmitry Mikheyev. 1987. xii, 88pp. $9.95.

ON GUARD FOR VICTORY: MILITARY DOCTRINE AND BALLISTIC MISSILE DEFENSE IN THE USSR. By Steven P. Adragna. 1987. xiv, 87pp. $9.95.

Special Reports

STRATEGIC MINERALS AND INTERNATIONAL SECURITY. Edited by Uri Ra'anan and Charles M. Perry. 1985. viii, 85pp. $9.95.

THIRD WORLD MARXIST-LENINIST REGIMES: STRENGTHS, VULNERABILITIES, AND U.S. POLICY. By Uri Ra'anan, Francis Fukuyama, Mark Falcoff, Sam C. Sarkesian, and Richard H. Shultz, Jr. 1985. xv, 125pp. $9.95.

THE RED ARMY ON PAKISTAN'S BORDER: POLICY IMPLICATIONS FOR THE UNITED STATES. By Anthony Arnold, Richard P. Cronin, Thomas Perry Thornton, Theodore L. Eliot, Jr., and Robert L. Pfaltzgraff, Jr. 1986. vi, 83pp. $9.95.

ASYMMETRIES IN U.S. AND SOVIET STRATEGIC DEFENSE PROGRAMS: IMPLICATIONS FOR NEAR-TERM AMERICAN DEPLOYMENT OPTIONS. By William A. Davis, Jr. 1986. xi, 71pp. $9.95.

REGIONAL SECURITY AND ANTI-TACTICAL BALLISTIC MISSILES: POLITICAL AND TECHNICAL ISSUES. By William A. Davis, Jr. 1986. xii, 54pp. $9.95.

NAVAL FORCES AND WESTERN SECURITY. By Francis J. West, Jr., Jacquelyn K. Davis, James E. Dougherty, Robert J. Hanks, and Charles M. Perry. 1987. xi, 55pp., Tables. $9.95.

DETERMINING FUTURE U.S. TACTICAL AIRLIFT REQUIREMENTS. By Jeffrey Record. 1987. vii, 40pp. $9.95.

NAVAL FORCES AND WESTERN SECURITY. By Francis J. West, Jr., Jacquelyn K. Davis, James E. Dougherty, Robert J. Hanks, and Charles M. Perry. 1987. xi, 56pp. $9.95.

NATO'S MARITIME STRATEGY: ISSUES AND DEVELOPMENTS. By E.F. Gueritz, Norman Friedman, Clarence A. Robinson, and William R. Van Cleave. 1987. xii, 79pp. $9.95.

NATO'S MARITIME FLANKS: PROBLEMS AND PROSPECTS. By H.F. Zeiner-Gundersen, Sergio A. Rossi, Marcel Duval, Donald C. Daniel, Gael D. Tarleton, and Milan Vego. 1987. xii, 119pp. $9.95.

SDI: HAS AMERICA TOLD HER STORY TO THE WORLD? By Dean Godson. Report of the IFPA Panel on Public Diplomacy. 1987. xviii, 67pp. $9.95.

BRITISH SECURITY POLICY AND THE ATLANTIC ALLIANCE: PROSPECTS FOR THE 1990s. By Martin Holmes, Gerald Frost, Christopher Coker, David Greenwood, Mark D.W. Edington, Dean Godson, Jacquelyn K. Davis, and Robert L. Pfaltzgraff, Jr. 1987. xv, 134pp. $9.95.

NICARAGUA V. UNITED STATES: A LOOK AT THE FACTS. By Robert F. Turner. 1987. xiv, 159pp. $9.95.

Books

ATLANTIC COMMUNITY IN CRISIS: A REDEFINITION OF THE ATLANTIC RELATIONSHIP. Edited by Walter F. Hahn and Robert L. Pfaltzgraff, Jr. 1979. 386pp. $43.00.

REVISING U.S. MILITARY STRATEGY: TAILORING MEANS TO ENDS. By Jeffrey Record. 1984. 113pp. $16.95 ($9.95, paper).

SHATTERING EUROPE'S DEFENSE CONSENSUS: THE ANTINUCLEAR PROTEST MOVEMENT AND THE FUTURE OF NATO. Edited by James E. Dougherty and Robert L. Pfaltzgraff, Jr. 1985. 226pp. $18.95.

INSTITUTE FOR FOREIGN POLICY ANALYSIS, INC.
List of Publications

Orders for the following titles in IFPA's series of Special Reports, Foreign Policy Reports, National Security Papers, Conference Reports, and Books should be addressed to the Circulation Manager, Institute for Foreign Policy Analysis, Central Plaza Building, Tenth Floor, 675 Massachusetts Avenue, Cambridge, Massachusetts 02139-3396. (Telephone: 617/492-2116.) Please send a check or money order for the correct amount together with your order.

Foreign Policy Reports

DEFENSE TECHNOLOGY AND THE ATLANTIC ALLIANCE: COMPETITION OR COLLABORATION? By Frank T.J. Bray and Michael Moodie. April 1977. vi, 42pp. $5.00.

IRAN'S QUEST FOR SECURITY: U.S. ARMS TRANSFERS AND THE NUCLEAR OPTION. By Alvin J. Cottrell and James E. Dougherty. May 1977. 59pp. $5.00.

ETHIOPIA, THE HORN OF AFRICA, AND U.S. POLICY. By John H. Spencer. September 1977. 69pp. $5.00.

BEYOND THE ARAB-ISRAELI SETTLEMENT: NEW DIRECTIONS FOR U.S. POLICY IN THE MIDDLE EAST. By R.K. Ramazani. September 1977. viii, 69pp. $5.00.

SPAIN, THE MONARCHY AND THE ATLANTIC COMMUNITY. By David C. Jordan. June 1979. v, 55pp. $5.00.

U.S. STRATEGY AT THE CROSSROADS: TWO VIEWS. By Robert J. Hanks and Jeffrey Record. July 1982. viii, 69pp. $7.50.

THE U.S. MILITARY PRESENCE IN THE MIDDLE EAST: PROBLEMS AND PROSPECTS. By Robert J. Hanks. December 1982. vii, 77pp. $7.50.

SOUTHERN AFRICA AND WESTERN SECURITY. By Robert J. Hanks. August 1983. vii, 71pp. $7.50.

THE WEST GERMAN PEACE MOVEMENT AND THE NATIONAL QUESTION. By Kim R. Holmes. March 1984. x, 73pp. $7.50.

THE HISTORY AND IMPACT OF MARXIST-LENINIST ORGANIZATIONAL THEORY. By John P. Roche. April 1984. x, 70pp. $7.50.

Special Reports

THE CRUISE MISSILE: BARGAINING CHIP OR DEFENSE BARGAIN? By Robert L. Pfaltzgraff, Jr., and Jacquelyn K. Davis. January 1977. x, 53pp. $3.00.

EUROCOMMUNISM AND THE ATLANTIC ALLIANCE. By James E. Dougherty and Diane K. Pfaltzgraff. January 1977. xiv, 66pp. $3.00.

THE NEUTRON BOMB: POLITICAL, TECHNICAL, AND MILITARY ISSUES. By S.T. Cohen. November 1978. xii, 95pp. $6.50.

SALT II AND U.S.-SOVIET STRATEGIC FORCES. By Jacquelyn K. Davis, Patrick J. Friel, and Robert L. Pfaltzgraff, Jr. June 1979. xii, 51pp. $5.00.

THE EMERGING STRATEGIC ENVIRONMENT: IMPLICATIONS FOR BALLISTIC MISSILE DEFENSE. By Leon Gouré, William G. Hyland, and Colin S. Gray. December 1979. xi, 75pp. $6.50.

THE SOVIET UNION AND BALLISTIC MISSILE DEFENSE. By Jacquelyn K. Davis, Uri Ra'anan, Robert L. Pfaltzgraff, Jr., Michael J. Deane, and John M. Collins. March 1980. xi, 71pp. $6.50. (Out of print).

ENERGY ISSUES AND ALLIANCE RELATIONSHIPS: THE UNITED STATES, WESTERN EUROPE AND JAPAN. By Robert L. Pfaltzgraff, Jr. April 1980. xii, 71pp. $6.50.

U.S. STRATEGIC-NUCLEAR POLICY AND BALLISTIC MISSILE DEFENSE: THE 1980S AND BEYOND. By William Schneider, Jr., Donald G. Brennan, William A. Davis, Jr., and Hans Rühle. April 1980. xii, 61pp. $6.50.

THE UNNOTICED CHALLENGE: SOVIET MARITIME STRATEGY AND THE GLOBAL CHOKE POINTS. By Robert J. Hanks. August 1980. xi, 66pp. $6.50.

FORCE REDUCTIONS IN EUROPE: STARTING OVER. By Jeffrey Record. October 1980. xi, 91pp. $6.50.

SALT II AND AMERICAN SECURITY. By Gordon J. Humphrey, William R. Van Cleave, Jeffrey Record, William H. Kincade, and Richard Perle. October 1980. xvi, 65pp.

THE FUTURE OF U.S. LAND-BASED STRATEGIC FORCES. By Jake Garn, J.I. Coffey, Lord Chalfont, and Ellery B. Block. December 1980. xvi, 80pp.

THE CAPE ROUTE: IMPERILED WESTERN LIFELINE. By Robert J. Hanks. February 1981. xi, 80pp. $6.50. (Hardcover, $10.00).

POWER PROJECTION AND THE LONG-RANGE COMBAT AIRCRAFT: MISSIONS, CAPABILITIES AND ALTERNATIVE DESIGNS. By Jacquelyn K. Davis and Robert L. Pfaltzgraff, Jr. June 1981. ix, 37pp. $6.50.

THE PACIFIC FAR EAST: ENDANGERED AMERICAN STRATEGIC POSITION. By Robert J. Hanks. October 1981. vii, 75pp. $7.50.

NATO'S THEATER NUCLEAR FORCE MODERNIZATION PROGRAM: THE REAL ISSUES. By Jeffrey Record. November 1981. viii, 102pp. $7.50.

THE CHEMISTRY OF DEFEAT: ASYMMETRIES IN U.S. AND SOVIET CHEMICAL WARFARE POSTURES. By Amoretta M. Hoeber. December 1981. xiii, 91pp. $6.50.

THE HORN OF AFRICA: A MAP OF POLITICAL-STRATEGIC CONFLICT. By James E. Dougherty. April 1982. xv, 74pp. $7.50.

THE WEST, JAPAN AND CAPE ROUTE IMPORTS: THE OIL AND NON-FUEL MINERAL TRADES. By Charles Perry. June 1982. xiv, 88pp. $7.50.

THE RAPID DEPLOYMENT FORCE AND U.S. MILITARY INTERVENTION IN THE PERSIAN GULF. By Jeffrey Record. May 1983, Second Edition. viii, 83pp. $7.50.

THE GREENS OF WEST GERMANY: ORIGINS, STRATEGIES, AND TRANSATLANTIC IMPLICATIONS. By Robert L. Pfaltzgraff, Jr., Kim R. Holmes, Clay Clemens, and Werner Kaltefleiter. August 1983. xi, 105pp. $7.50.

THE ATLANTIC ALLIANCE AND U.S. GLOBAL STRATEGY. By Jacquelyn K. Davis and Robert L. Pfaltzgraff, Jr. September 1983. x, 44pp. $7.50.

WORLD ENERGY SUPPLY AND INTERNATIONAL SECURITY. By Herman Franssen, John P. Hardt, Jacquelyn K. Davis, Robert J. Hanks, Charles Perry, Robert L. Pfaltzgraff, Jr., and Jeffrey Record. October 1983. xiv, 93pp. $7.50.

POISONING ARMS CONTROL: THE SOVIET UNION AND CHEMICAL/BIOLOGICAL WEAPONS. By Mark C. Storella. June 1984. xi, 99pp. $7.50.

National Security Papers

CBW: THE POOR MAN'S ATOMIC BOMB. By Neil C. Livingstone and Joseph D. Douglass, Jr., with a Foreword by Senator John Tower. February 1984. x, 33pp. $5.00.

U.S. STRATEGIC AIRLIFT: REQUIREMENTS AND CAPABILITIES. By Jeffrey Record. January 1986. vi, 38pp. $6.00.

STRATEGIC BOMBERS: HOW MANY ARE ENOUGH? By Jeffrey Record. January 1986. vi, 22pp. $6.00.

STRATEGIC DEFENSE AND EXTENDED DETERRENCE: A NEW TRANSATLANTIC DEBATE. By Jacquelyn K. Davis and Robert L. Pfaltzgraff, Jr. February 1986. viii, 51pp. $8.00.

JCS REORGANIZATION AND U.S. ARMS CONTROL POLICY. By James E. Dougherty. March 1986. xiv, 27pp. $6.00.

STRATEGIC FORCE MODERNIZATION AND ARMS CONTROL. Contributions by Edward L. Rowny, R. James Woolsey, Harold Brown, Alexander M. Haig, Jr., Albert Gore, Jr., Brent Scowcroft, Russell E. Dougherty, A. Casey, Gordon Fornell, and Sam Nunn. 1986. xiii, 43pp. $6.00.

U.S. BOMBER FORCE MODERNIZATION. Contributions by Mike Synar, Richard K. Betts, William Kaufmann, Russell E. Dougherty, Richard DeLauer, and Dan Quayle. 1986. vii, 9pp. $5.00.

U.S. STRATEGIC AIRLIFT CHOICES. Contributions by William S. Cohen, Russell Murray, Frederick G. Kroesen, William Kaufmann, Harold Brown, James A. Courter, and Robert W. Komer. 1986. ix, 13pp. $5.00.

Books

SOVIET MILITARY STRATEGY IN EUROPE. By Joseph D. Douglass, Jr. Pergamon Press, 1980. 252pp. (Out of print).

THE WARSAW PACT: ARMS, DOCTRINE, AND STRATEGY. By William J. Lewis. New York: McGraw-Hill Publishing Co., 1982. 471pp. $15.00.

THE BISHOPS AND NUCLEAR WEAPONS: THE CATHOLIC PASTORAL LETTER ON WAR AND PEACE. By James E. Dougherty. Archon Books, 1984. 255pp. $22.50.

Conference Reports

NATO AND ITS FUTURE: A GERMAN-AMERICAN ROUNDTABLE. Summary of a Dialogue. 1978. 22pp. $1.00.

SECOND GERMAN-AMERICAN ROUNDTABLE ON NATO: THE THEATER-NUCLEAR BALANCE. 1978. 32pp. $1.00.

THE SOVIET UNION AND BALLISTIC MISSILE DEFENSE. 1978. 26pp. $1.00.

U.S. STRATEGIC-NUCLEAR POLICY AND BALLISTIC MISSILE DEFENSE: THE 1980S AND BEYOND. 1979. 30pp. $1.00.

SALT II AND AMERICAN SECURITY. 1979. 39pp.

THE FUTURE OF U.S. LAND-BASED STRATEGIC FORCES. 1979. 32pp. $1.00.

THE FUTURE OF NUCLEAR POWER. 1980. 48pp. $1.00.

THIRD GERMAN-AMERICAN ROUNDTABLE ON NATO: MUTUAL AND BALANCED FORCE REDUCTIONS IN EUROPE. 1980. 27pp. $1.00.

FOURTH GERMAN-AMERICAN ROUNDTABLE ON NATO: NATO MODERNIZATION AND EUROPEAN SECURITY. 1981. 15pp. $1.00.

SECOND ANGLO-AMERICAN SYMPOSIUM ON DETERRENCE AND EUROPEAN SECURITY. 1981. 25pp. $1.00.

THE U.S. DEFENSE MOBILIZATION INFRASTRUCTURE: PROBLEMS AND PRIORITIES. The Tenth Annual Conference, sponsored by the International Security Studies Program, The Fletcher School of Law and Diplomacy, Tufts University. 1981. 25pp. $1.00.

U.S. STRATEGIC DOCTRINE FOR THE 1980S. 1982. 14pp.

FRENCH-AMERICAN SYMPOSIUM ON STRATEGY, DETERRENCE AND EUROPEAN SECURITY. 1982. 14pp. $1.00.

FIFTH GERMAN-AMERICAN ROUNDTABLE ON NATO: THE CHANGING CONTEXT OF THE EUROPEAN SECURITY DEBATE. Summary of a Transatlantic Dialogue. 1982. 22pp. $1.00.

ENERGY SECURITY AND THE FUTURE OF NUCLEAR POWER. 1982. 39pp. $2.50.

INTERNATIONAL SECURITY DIMENSIONS OF SPACE. The Eleventh Annual Conference, sponsored by the International Security Studies Program, The Fletcher School of Law and Diplomacy, Tufts University. 1982. 24pp. $2.50.

PORTUGAL, SPAIN AND TRANSATLANTIC RELATIONS. Summary of a Transatlantic Dialogue. 1983. 18pp. $2.50.

JAPANESE-AMERICAN SYMPOSIUM ON REDUCING STRATEGIC MINERALS VULNERABILITIES: CURRENT PLANS, PRIORITIES, AND POSSIBILITIES FOR COOPERATION. 1983. 31pp. $2.50.

NATIONAL SECURITY POLICY: THE DECISION-MAKING PROCESS. The Twelfth Annual Conference, sponsored by the International Security Studies Program, The Fletcher School of Law and Diplomacy, Tufts University. 1983. 28pp. $2.50.

THE SECURITY OF THE ATLANTIC, IBERIAN AND NORTH AFRICAN REGIONS. Summary of a Transatlantic Dialogue. 1983. 25pp. $2.50.

THE WEST EUROPEAN ANTINUCLEAR PROTEST MOVEMENT: IMPLICATIONS FOR WESTERN SECURITY. Summary of a Transatlantic Dialogue. 1984. 21pp. $2.50.

THE U.S.-JAPANESE SECURITY RELATIONSHIP IN TRANSITION. Summary of a Transpacific Dialogue. 1984. 23pp. $2.50.

SIXTH GERMAN-AMERICAN ROUNDTABLE ON NATO: NATO AND EUROPEAN SECURITY—BEYOND INF. Summary of a Transatlantic Dialogue. 1984. 31pp. $2.50.

SECURITY COMMITMENTS AND CAPABILITIES: ELEMENTS OF AN AMERICAN GLOBAL STRATEGY. The Thirteenth Annual Conference, sponsored by the International Security Studies Program, The Fletcher School of Law and Diplomacy, Tufts University. 1984. 21pp. $2.50.

THIRD JAPANESE-AMERICAN-GERMAN CONFERENCE ON THE FUTURE OF NUCLEAR ENERGY. 1984. 40pp. $2.50.

SEVENTH GERMAN-AMERICAN ROUNDTABLE ON NATO: POLITICAL CONSTRAINTS, EMERGING TECHNOLOGIES, AND ALLIANCE STRATEGY. Summary of a Transatlantic Dialogue. 1985. 36pp. $2.50.

TERRORISM AND OTHER "LOW-INTENSITY" OPERATIONS: INTERNATIONAL LINKAGES. The Fourteenth Annual Conference, sponsored by the International Security Studies Program, The Fletcher School of Law and Diplomacy, Tufts University. 1985. 21pp. $2.50.

EAST-WEST TRADE AND TECHNOLOGY TRANSFER: NEW CHALLENGES FOR THE UNITED STATES. Second Annual Forum, co-sponsored by the Institute for Foreign Policy Analysis and the International Security Studies Program, The Fletcher School of Law and Diplomacy, Tufts University. 1986. 40pp. $3.50.

ORGANIZING FOR NATIONAL SECURITY: THE ROLE OF THE JOINT CHIEFS OF STAFF. 1986. 32pp. $2.50.

EIGHTH GERMAN-AMERICAN ROUNDTABLE ON NATO: STRATEGIC DEFENSE, NATO MODERNIZATION, AND EAST-WEST RELATIONS. Summary of a Transatlantic Dialogue. 1986. 47pp. $2.50.

EMERGING DOCTRINES AND TECHNOLOGIES: IMPLICATIONS FOR GLOBAL AND REGIONAL POLITICAL-MILITARY BALANCES. The Fifteenth Annual Conference, sponsored by the International Security Studies Program, The Fletcher School of Law and Diplomacy, Tufts University. 1986. 49pp. $2.50.

STRATEGIC WAR TERMINATION: POLITICAL-MILITARY-DIPLOMATIC DIMENSIONS. 1986. 22pp. $2.50.

SDI AND EUROPEAN SECURITY: ENHANCING CONVENTIONAL DEFENSE. 1987. 21pp. $2.50.

STRATEGIC DEFENSE: INDUSTRIAL APPLICATIONS AND POLITICAL IMPLICATIONS. 1987. ix, 29pp. $2.50.

THE FUTURE OF NATO FORCES. 1987. ix, 30pp. $2.50.